■ SCHOLASTIC

Pairing Fiction
& Nonfiction

Deanne Camp

NEW YORK • TORONTO • LONDON • AUCKLAND • SYDNEY
MEXICO CITY • NEW DELHI • HONG KONG • BUENOS AIRES

Teaching *Resources*

Dedication
I dedicate this book to:
- Dave, my loving husband
- Stacie and Melissa, my beautiful daughters
- Jared and Grace, my windows onto the excitement of literacy development

Acknowledgments
- Thank you to the Reading Faculty at Missouri State University for their constant support
- Thank you to Jeanette Moss for her encouragement and patience throughout this work
- Thank you to the teachers in southwest Missouri who shared part of their lives with me and allowed me the freedom to create a mosaic of educators

Cover design by Maria Lilja
Interior design by Melinda Belter
Photos by Deanne Camp

Editing by Jeanette Moss and Shoshana Wolfe

ISBN-13 978-0-439-29708-0
ISBN-10 0-439-29708-7

2 3 4 5 6 7 8 9 10   31   14 13 12 11 10 09 08 07 06

Contents

CHAPTER 4

Twin-Book Strategies to Enhance Writing

Introduction

I HAVE ALWAYS USED CHILDREN'S LITERATURE IN MY TEACHING BECAUSE BOOKS WRITTEN FOR CHILDREN HAVE ALWAYS BEEN AND WILL CONTINUE TO BE MY PASSION. However, my love for reading great literature to my students did not alone create a successful reading and writing program in my classroom. It has taken many years of teaching at the elementary school and university levels to successfully incorporate my love of children's literature into a broader approach to teaching. This approach relies on using "twin books"—one fiction and one nonfiction—that relate to each other in content. It spans the curriculum and motivates students to enjoy reading and weave ideas from fiction and nonfiction into their content-area learning.

I began as an inexperienced first-grade teacher reading aloud children's literature classics and introducing trade books to supplement the required basal series. For example, when only snippets of A. A. Milne's *Winnie the Pooh* or Arnold Lobel's Frog and Toad series were included in my basal readers, I shared with students the "real," full-length story. I knew I was on to something because of the enthusiasm with which students responded to authentic literature, but I had not yet learned to integrate into other areas of the curriculum the rich trade books my students and I loved.

As I grew more comfortable using both trade books and the content textbooks, I began to supplement textbooks in other curriculum areas with related fiction books. During a third-grade social studies unit on westward expansion, for example, I paired the textbook with fiction books such as the Laura Ingalls Wilder's Little House series and Patricia MacLachlan's *Sarah, Plain and Tall*. Students listened or followed along enthusiastically in their copies during daily Read Alouds. Driven by their deep interest in the lives of the characters, the setting details, and the problems these characters faced, students wrote a play set in the 1800s. They chose cast members, wrote set directions, created props, and videotaped the play to share with parents and other classes in our building. We even built a covered wagon, using a table, a step stool, cardboard, several bedsheets, flexible tubing, and lots of imagination. It was clear to me that using the textbook alone wouldn't have sparked the same fascination for learning about the early settlers that using the fiction and nonfiction books along with it did.

I also began to see how nonfiction books with lots of fascinating details could serve as an important teaching tool—they could answer specific questions raised by fiction books that usually could not be answered by the general information in textbooks. In the same westward expansion unit, we read Ellen Levine's *If You Traveled West in a Covered Wagon* and Russell Freedman's *Children of the Wild West*. While we were videotaping the play about early settlers, the four students who volunteered to sit under the covered wagon (table) and turn the cardboard wheels realized that they wanted to know more about wagon wheels and how they rotate. Finding answers to students' questions about covered-wagons and wagon-wheel construction was a perfect reason to study nonfiction books that include details not found in the textbook. Our nonfiction reading also helped us answer other questions students raised from their work with the fiction texts: *Why do wagon wheels sometimes look as if they are turning backwards? When the wagon turns a corner, do all four wheels turn around the same number of times and at the same speed?*

Since my own teaching days, I've continued to develop ways to pair fiction and nonfiction books to enrich students' learning and help teachers meet both literacy and content-area objectives in literature-based lessons. My twin-book approach offers teachers a practical, manageable way to plan instruction and at the same time enables students to delve deep in an area of particular interest. In fact, working with twin books is a great way to incorporate vocabulary, comprehension, and writing strategies that help students acquire key background knowledge and spark their interest in learning more about the topic or unit of study. As students learn how to work with and compare multiple sources, they build the skills they need for text analysis and researching—skills they'll need for their studies in middle school, high school, and beyond.

I've been privileged to work side by side with a number of teachers to develop the strategy lessons in this book. I thank them and hope that you'll find their lessons and classroom examples useful—and that you'll be inspired to use them as models for creating your own twin-book lessons.

CHAPTER 1

Getting Started

What Are Twin Books?

Twin books are two books—one fiction and one nonfiction—on related topics. They are used together to introduce and reinforce content-area material while targeting key language-arts skills. With twin books you can easily integrate language arts with science, social studies, and math in an exciting way. You'll avoid relying solely on textbooks with those often dry passages written specifically to relate general facts or teach a strategy or skill. Most important, using twin books as part of your teaching motivates students to learn.

I work in a second- and third-grade classroom with a teacher who has designed a rain forest unit that fascinates the students. She relies only partially on the social studies textbook—it offers only a short section on the destruction of rain forest land and creatures. Last year, the teacher chose twin books to enhance this unit and help her students learn more about the rain forest ecosystem and how to be good stewards of our planet. She first shared the nonfiction book *The Rain Forest* by René Mettler and Jean Marzollo, and students readily absorbed facts about the endangered environment and the vocabulary to describe it. They were intrigued by the book's transparent overlays, which make the illustrations appear almost real. Next, she read aloud the fiction book *The Great Kapok Tree* by Lynne Cherry. After hearing this book, the children wrote letters to the Children's Rain Forest, an organization dedicated to environmental protection cited in the book. Through rereading, referring to the textbook for support, and discussing what they'd learned in peer and class discussions, they not only learned the unit content and related vocabulary but were able to put that learning to use in meaningful ways: They became more concerned about local environmental issues and took up the cause of safeguarding green space in their own community.

Why Pair Fiction and Nonfiction Books?

- *To meet academic standards.* Pairing fiction and nonfiction trade books on the same or similar topics can help you meet all your school district's curricular goals (often based on the national standards for each content area).

- *To get students excited about learning.* When you choose twin books from the outstanding array of children's literature and informational books available today, content-area material can come alive. Students attend with greater interest and focus to the information presented, which helps them retain what they learn and certainly makes learning more meaningful and enjoyable than following the traditional drill of reading a textbook chapter and answering the questions at the end.

- *To develop students' background knowledge.* A reader's background knowledge may be the single most important factor in his or her ability to learn from texts. And students need to learn ways to connect new information to what they already know. However, many students lack the necessary background knowledge to understand content-area textbooks. Using twin books helps you present new information in appealing ways so that students can absorb it more easily. Reading with twin books is often introduced as an appetizer to the unit of study: Students read or listen to and interact with these texts prior to their textbook reading and familiarize themselves with vocabulary and concepts they'll need to read the textbook and other sources of information.

- *To increase students' vocabulary.* Working with twin books increases students' vocabulary by encouraging them to discuss with their peers specific, detailed information about the topic they're studying. The more students want to know about a topic, the more words they need to know.

- *To improve students' comprehension.* As knowledge, ownership, and usage of new vocabulary increases, so does comprehension. Because twin books keep students fascinated, focused on the topic, and eager to use new vocabulary to discuss what they've learned, comprehension—the main purpose of reading—improves.

- *To improve students' critical thinking skills.* Students who engage with twin books go far beyond simply decoding a string of words across a line of print; they want to ask questions and find answers about what they've read, so they compare, synthesize, and evaluate information across texts, building comprehension through critical thinking.

- *To enhance students' writing.* Reading and writing go hand in hand; students become better writers by writing extensively about topics that interest them, just as they become better readers by reading extensively about topics that interest them. You can use twin books to extend writing activities in exciting ways, engaging students in writing about high-interest topics they've encountered in their reading. And as they present information in a new way through their writing, they work with the ideas, words, and phrases the author uses. This process of writing builds students' word recognition and critical thinking abilities.

- *To help you meet the dual goals of presenting content-area information and exposing students to excellent literature.* Over the past several years, readers have been treated to an explosion of high-quality books published for children—both fiction and nonfiction. Choosing two books to compare and contrast is a great way to maintain your content focus as well as meet literacy goals. You can share literature with students in a variety of formats, including Read Aloud, shared reading, guided reading, literature circles, partner and small-group reading, and independent reading. As you use the books to help students gain content knowledge, you will also be able to teach key literacy concepts—from using context to determine word meaning to genre and literary elements.

Twin Books Help Students
Understand the Textbook

Students often struggle with content-area material, particularly in the assigned textbook, because the text is densely written. By contrast, most students easily recognize the story structures of fiction books, since most have had a wide range of experience with narrative texts in the primary grades at school, through teacher Read Alouds and shared-book experiences, and during independent reading time.

Many writers of children's nonfiction have also begun to use a more engaging narrative tone and to incorporate some narrative patterns that grab students' attention and help them make connections with the material more readily. Students love to read these books because they can offer a wealth of detailed factual information through a style that appeals to them.

Reading well-written fiction and nonfiction books on the same topic can help students warm up to the textbook. Having read and interacted with the twin books, they approach the textbook with increased confidence and more background knowledge on which to build.

Using Twin Books
in Your Classroom

When you use twin books in your lessons, be sure to choose the two books carefully (see the FAQ section below). Then decide which book—fiction or nonfiction—to introduce first. You may vary the order according to the books you've selected, your lesson requirements, and your students' needs.

If you're reading the books aloud, I recommend introducing the fiction book first to encourage students' initial exploration of a topic and enhance their interest in the nonfiction twin book. Once they've heard the story, they'll be ready and eager for the facts offered in the nonfiction book. The fiction book will provide some background knowledge and serve as a prelude to the factual information students will read in the textbook. Of course, if you find that your students gravitate to the photos, captions, charts, and other features of a nonfiction selection, you may want to lead with the nonfiction book.

If you are using a class set of the twin books, you may want to introduce both books at the same time, "pitching" each book with a commercial-style book talk. Then invite students to choose which book to read first. (This approach requires careful planning in order to provide support for struggling readers who may need help with one or both of the twin books.)

Provide structured and unstructured time for students to respond to their books—on their own, in pairs, and in groups. You'll find many suggestions for a variety of reading response activities and formats in the following chapters. After students have spent time developing prior knowledge and vocabulary from the paired books, have them focus on the content knowledge found in the textbook. For example, a fifth-grade teacher in a classroom I recently visited discovered that his students more easily learned and retained the densely written information about the Civil War in the social studies textbook when they first read the twin books *Thunder on the Tennessee* by G. Clifton Wisler and *A Nation Torn: The Story of How the Civil War Began* by Delia Ray (see Lesson 4). After several days of comparing and discussing the texts, creating individual vocabulary lists, and using a graphic organizer to sort information, students were able to use the textbook both to confirm information that they had already read and to answer some questions that hadn't been answered in the twin books; they were informed and excited.

Choosing Twin Books: FAQs

Do I need to have a class set of copies in order to use twin books?
Having multiple copies of each twin-book title would be ideal but often isn't realistic in terms of budget. Don't let that deter you from using twin books. If you have only one or a few copies of a book, you may want to use this book as the lead-in Read Aloud for a lesson or unit. You may also have students browse through and pass around a single copy during independent reading and later select a short section to read aloud.

What if the twin books I select are written at different reading levels?
Twin books need not be on the same reading level. In fact, you can use differently leveled books—independent, instructional, or challenging—quite effectively. A very challenging text may work as a Read Aloud or as a partner-read book, with students focusing on a specific section. An easier book may be one that most students can read independently while you support struggling readers in a guided-reading group. You may also want students to practice and read aloud short selections from an independent reading–level book to the class so that they can improve fluent oral reading. For example, independent, or easy, twin books on the Civil War for fifth graders may include *Pink and Say* by Patricia Polacco (fiction) and *If You Traveled on the Underground Railroad* by Ellen Levine (nonfiction). More challenging twin books might include the ones used in Lesson 4: Wisler's *Thunder on the Tennessee* (fiction) and Ray's *A Nation Torn* (nonfiction).

Must I always choose a realistic fiction book as my fiction text?
Certainly not. The fiction book may come from a wide range of genres, including fantasy, folktale, or myth. Students can learn about these genres as they discuss the differences in structure and purpose between the twin books.

How do I make sure the twin books I've chosen are a good match?
Compare side by side the two books you're considering and make sure that they

- support your lesson objectives and expand on information in the content textbook.

- match well in content and vocabulary. If the books contain similar vocabulary, students will be exposed to new words in different contexts—a powerful way to reinforce vocabulary knowledge.

- have a structure that promotes learning concepts instead of isolated facts. For example, *A Picture of Freedom: The Diary of Clotee, a Slave Girl* by Patricia McKissack (fiction) and the autobiography *Rosa Parks: My Story* (nonfiction) from Lesson 3 both contain factual information, but the underlying themes clearly focus on the experience of African Americans during the Civil War and the 1950s and 1960s.

- contain excellent examples of language. They should include standard English (or another language, such as Spanish) and authentic examples of cultural language usage. *A Picture of Freedom: The Diary of Clotee, a Slave Girl,* for example, uses dialect and strong narrative voice to convey information about slavery.

- include illustrations or artwork that is of outstanding quality and appropriate for the text.

- contain visual information, such as charts and graphs, that is accurate and adds to the knowledge base.

What else should I consider when choosing twin books?
Above all, consider the appropriateness of the books in light of your students' ages and developmental levels: Should you use picture books to teach both content and skills? Also consider the amount of time you have to work with the books: Do you have time to read chapter books? Or, because of time constraints, should you read a short story or key sections of a book?

Most twin books used by the grades 3–5 teachers in the examples in this book are well known and readily available in book stores and online. If you happen to be teaching a topic addressed in a sample lesson, you may want to substitute books you already have in your classroom or ones better matched to the lives and needs of your students.

Using the Lessons in This Book

Before you use the lessons in the following chapters, be sure students understand that authors may choose from a variety of text structures in their writing. You may want to present a mini-lesson on the difference between fiction and nonfiction. Explain that most fiction texts are narrative stories driven by a plotline and have a well-defined beginning, middle, and ending. In contrast, the structure of nonfiction, or expository, material may not present material sequentially from beginning to end. The structure affects the way we read a book. In general, fiction texts must be read from beginning to end. But with non-fiction books, students can focus on those portions of text most meaningful to the topic of study.

Let's look at a mini-lesson that illustrates the differences between fiction and nonfiction with the twin books from Lesson 1, *Postcards From Pluto: A Tour of the Solar System* by Loreen Leedy (fiction) and *Do Stars Have Points?* by Melvin and Gilda Berger (nonfiction).

- *Introduce the twin books.* Ask students: *Which book looks as though its purpose is strictly informative—to present facts? Which book is likely fiction, containing parts that may be story-like and not based on facts?* Students may answer that the title *Postcards*

From Pluto sounds unrealistic because no humans have ever been to Pluto. *Do Stars Have Points?* on the other hand, suggests that someone will be answering questions and dispelling myths we may have about outer space. Students may also note that the illustrations on the *Do Stars Have Points?* cover look more realistic than the cartoon-style illustrations on the *Postcards From Pluto* cover.

- ***Explain that the fiction book contains some facts along the way but is basically a story.*** Show students that *Postcards From Pluto* has a story text structure: a definite beginning (*the kids in the story take off on a Space Tours Inc. shuttle*), middle (*the kids visit the planets in sequence and write a postcard home from each*), and end (*they head back to Earth and write a final postcard that defines some of the new terms they've learned*).

- ***Talk about the fact that the nonfiction book contains only factual material.*** Compare the beginning of *Do Stars Have Points?* with that of *Postcards From Pluto*: Instead of setting up a story line with characters, the nonfiction book launches right into an answer to the title question. The text continues in a question-and-answer format to present lots of useful information on stars, planets, and outer space. In addition, it has a table of contents, an index, charts, and realistic illustrations to provide you with additional information.

- ***Show that fiction books must be read straight through but nonfiction can be picked up anywhere and make sense.*** For example with *Postcards From Pluto,* the reader won't understand why the kids are in outer space unless he or she begins at the beginning. With *Do Stars Have Points?* the reader may open the book to almost any page, find an interesting question, such as "Do the planets move?" and read an informative explanation. They may also use the index to find precisely the information they need.

The following chapters show how to integrate language-arts strategies with fiction and nonfiction twin books to improve content-area comprehension in your classroom. The chapters include strategies to improve vocabulary, comprehension, and writing. Each chapter includes teacher-tested lessons for several sets of twin books, and each lesson plan highlights how to use a specific strategy or technique to enhance the unit or area of study. You can apply the focus strategies to any of the twin books mentioned or to other children's literature choices that fit your curricular objectives.

Let's begin with twin-book strategies that help build vocabulary and word ownership.

CHAPTER 2

Twin-Book Strategies to Boost Word-Identification and Word-Ownership Skills

Teachers must help students make the connection between word recognition and comprehension . . . [by] offering interesting literature at their level.

—Hurst, Wilson, Camp, & Cramer, *Creating Independent Readers* (2002)

Comprehension is, of course, the goal of reading any type of text material—books, newspapers, magazines, and so on. To comprehend written material, students need to gain ownership of a body of words and acquire strategies to help them recognize words quickly and accurately. In the 1985 report *Becoming a Nation of Readers*, the Commission on Reading notes that "one of the cornerstones of skilled reading is fast, accurate word identification," a view supported by recent phonics and fluency research cited in the 2000 *Report of the National Reading Panel*. Yet the aim of teaching word identification and word ownership strategies is to enable students to read and *understand* written text, not simply to decode words across a line of print. So students need vocabulary instruction that includes not only repeated exposure to new words through reading, but also opportunities to use these words meaningfully in discussions and in writing. When students have a firm grasp of a text's vocabulary, they focus more on meaning and less on decoding.

The five strategies presented in this chapter offer students opportunities to manipulate, compare, categorize, and write with vocabulary from the twin books you choose. The lessons are designed to increase students' interactions with and learning from texts. Twin books provide an authentic way to capture and hold students' interest in the topic area while they absorb new words—from basic, topic-related vocabulary to more challenging words that describe concepts and themes.

WORD SORT
Hands-on Experience With Words Empowers Readers

OBJECTIVE

To increase the number of content-related words students can comprehend when listening and use when speaking and writing

HOW IT WORKS

A word sort is a vocabulary development strategy in which students group selected words into categories in order to strengthen word identification and ownership (Gillet & Kita, 1979). *Closed* word sorts focus students' attention on a single language characteristic (for example, syllables, vowel sounds, patterns, or word structure); *open* word sorts require students to decide how individual words relate to the topic addressed in the reading selections.

When categorizing words, students have the opportunity to activate prior word knowledge as well as gain ownership of new vocabulary. Sorting words according to language characteristics helps students learn how those words are constructed and to pronounce and spell them correctly. When developing the categories themselves during an open sort, students need to use higher-order cognitive skills and focus on the meaning of words. In this lesson, students use both sorting strategies to build ownership of words used in the twin books.

WHEN TO USE WORD SORTS

■ Before Reading

Using a word sort with words taken from a text before reading helps to activate prior knowledge and build background. After completing the activity, students will be able to draw on the key terms they've learned to more efficiently read the twin books and any supplementary textbook material; they may also use the words in teacher-chosen categories to predict what the reading selections will be about.

■ After Reading

After reading, a word sort helps to clarify definitions of vocabulary words used in the reading selections. Posting completed word sorts for the remainder of the study helps students retain new vocabulary and take responsibility for checking their own spelling.

PUTTING THE STRATEGY INTO ACTION

The examples in the following lesson come from an integrated travel unit developed for third graders by Melissa Messina. The final segment of the unit, which includes the study of planets, stars, and other celestial objects, requires students to integrate a significant amount of vocabulary. Although her students have heard many of the words before, they do not necessarily know their meanings or how to spell them. Messina uses twin books Do Stars Have Points? *and* Postcards From Pluto: A Tour of the Solar System. *(For more on Messina's unit, see page 18.)*

1. *Select the twin books.* Choose a nonfiction book that provides students with plenty of exposure to curriculum-related vocabulary as well as opportunities to research word meanings by investigating the text, glossary, and illustrations when necessary. Be sure to choose a book with vocabulary that appropriately challenges both struggling readers and those who are more accomplished and confident.

   Pair this text with a work of fiction that provides students with additional exposure to and practice with the vocabulary in the nonfiction text. The vocabulary should occur naturally in the context of a narrative students are likely to find compelling and memorable.

2. *Begin with either an open or closed sort and continue with one of the processes below.* Use a closed sort to focus students' attention closely on one language characteristic at a time; use an open sort to give students an opportunity to investigate word meanings and their relationship to the topic. Plan to do both types of word sorts in the context of a unit of study. To model the word sort, draw a simple chart with the same number of columns as you have categories. Students may copy the chart on notebook paper and fill it in on their own.

   ## CLOSED SORT
   a. **Before introducing the twin books, choose from the reading selections words that students need to know to comprehend the text.** The words Messina chooses from the twin books are ones her third graders often see in science textbooks as well as in newspapers, magazines, and other reading material both in and out of school. The word list for this activity includes the following terms:

solar	star	galaxy	revolve	rotate	outer space
gravity	comet	light-year	constellation	planets	craters
asteroid	orbit	hemisphere	Milky Way		

   b. **Choose two or more categories into which you want students to sort the words.** Messina completes two closed word sorts to give students enough practice with the focus words that they feel a sense of ownership of the vocabulary.

For the first she chooses the number of syllables. She likes the syllable sort because her students need practice in chunking words (breaking them into meaningful parts). The second closed sort stresses vowel usage. Both exercises reinforce correct spelling of the focus words.

1 syllable	2 syllables	3 syllables	4 syllables
STAR	SOLAR	GALAXY	CONSTELLATION
	LIGHT-YEAR	MILKY WAY	
	PLANETS	HEMISPHERE	
	REVOLVE	GRAVITY	
	ORBIT	OUTER SPACE	
	ROTATE	ASTEROID	
	COMET		
	CRATERS		

long a	long e	long i	long o
CONSTELLATION	REVOLVE	LIGHT-YEAR	SOLAR
ROTATE	HEMISPHERE		ROTATE
CRATERS	GRAVITY		
MILKY WAY	GALAXY		
OUTER SPACE	MILKY WAY		

c. **Discuss each list of words and why it is placed in its category.** Messina's students like big words, so those with three or four syllables are usually the ones they learn first and most easily identify in the twin books.

OPEN SORT

a. **Use the same list of words for the open sort.** Messina uses an open sort to make sure students know the meaning of each word—not just how to pronounce it.

b. **Work individually, in small groups, or even with the whole class to have students create their own categories.** Each of Messina's five groups use the list of words to come up with the categories as well as an explanation for the other groups about why they chose them. Students usually offer good reasons for choosing one heading or category over another.

c. **Allow time for a class discussion to explain category headings.** Messina asks each group to choose one list to share with class members. Here are three group-created open sorts for the space-travel words.

Objects often seen in the sky (without a telescope)
STAR
CONSTELLATION
PLANETS

Largest to smallest
SOLAR SYSTEM
MILKY WAY
STARS
SUN
PLANETS
EARTH

Makes us think of Earth
GRAVITY
REVOLVE
ORBIT
ROTATE
PLANETS

3. *Evaluate.* Design follow-up activities for your students that require them to use their newly expanded vocabulary. Writing letters to a local newspaper, business, or organization; illustrating posters or informational brochures; and scripting plays allow students to demonstrate their learning in a meaningful context. Give students a list (or a target number) of vocabulary words they will need to use and spell correctly, and review their assignments for accuracy. Monitor students' speech and writing for the presence, appropriate use, and correct spelling of the vocabulary words encountered in the twin books.

Strategy Spotlight: **WORD SORT**

The Twin Books:

FICTION

Postcards From Pluto:
A Tour of the Solar System
by Loreen Leedy
(Scholastic, 1993)

Mr. Quasar, a robot, takes a group of children on a tour of our solar system. The children write postcards to their families at home on Earth sharing information about objects they see on their out-of-this-world tour.

NONFICTION

Do Stars Have Points?
by Melvin and Gilda Berger
(Scholastic, 1998)

Questions asked and answered in this book are ones curious children might ask about stars and planets. The simple question-and-answer format and colorful illustrations make it easy for children to find the answers to their questions. For more difficult words, the book includes pronunciation clues.

■ Classroom Context

Messina begins her annual travel unit with the history of travel and ends with travel modes of the future. During this portion of the unit, Messina's students use their twin books to learn about outer space and space travel. The twin books she chooses provide her students with an engaging context for learning important vocabulary, facts, and concepts, as well as a format—postcards—for a follow-up project.

■ Why These Twin Books?

Messina introduces her students to *Postcards from Pluto: A Tour of the Solar System* as a follow-up to an earlier activity that involved writing letters to travel agencies. *Do Stars Have Points*? is an excellent

nonfiction companion because it answers many questions her students always ask during the space-travel study. The book also includes vocabulary her third graders need to master.

■ How the Strategy Activity Fits In

Messina's fiction twin book, *Postcards From Pluto*, is a picture book that incorporates the travel theme and pictures student characters writing. After reading the book (and studying the nonfiction text), students create postcards modeled on those in the book. Messina's students recognize that their writing space on postcards will be limited; therefore, they will need to choose their words carefully. Sorting the words encountered in the twin books gives her students a command of the vocabulary they need to complete this follow-up activity skillfully.

Messina's students have more opportunities to demonstrate their learning through two additional art projects, paper-bag books (see below) and shadow boxes, and the accompanying writing that explains them to viewers. Her third graders work in small groups or independently to create projects reflective of what they've learned.

■ Success Story

Messina's students use the vocabulary words they learned from the twin-book word sorts on their postcards, in the paper-bag books, and on information cards attached to the shadow boxes. Messina notes that students use the vocabulary words with more ease and apparent understanding as they work on the culminating projects for the outer-space section of the travel unit.

PREDICT-O-GRAM
Word Relationships Build a Context for Reading

OBJECTIVE
To help students determine how important words and terms relate to the story in a fiction book and to the main topic of study in a nonfiction book

HOW IT WORKS
Predict-O-Grams are a tried-and-true tool for helping students acquire new vocabulary and find relationships among words by organizing them into meaningful categories (Blochowicz, 1986).

Using Predict-O-Grams with twin books can help pique students' curiosity about a topic of study. Students group words into teacher-made categories and read the fiction book to find out whether their predictions about word meanings are correct; then they apply their new word knowledge as they read and discuss the nonfiction book.

WHEN TO USE PREDICT-O-GRAMS
Though they can be used flexibly, Predict-O-Grams are most effective when they are begun before reading and completed after reading.

■ Before Reading
Predict-O-Grams acquaint students with vocabulary in a reading selection prior to their reading. By carefully selecting categories and key words related to the book's structure and content, you can help students organize the words meaningfully. They should begin to see word relationships that help them predict important events and concepts.

■ After Reading
Students look at the Predict-O-Gram charts they completed (individually or as a group) to confirm or refute earlier predictions about which categories the vocabulary words best fit into. By discussing their decisions about where to place the words, students determine whether they understand the meaning of a word and how it functions in the book. Then they are able to use these words in other contexts.

PUTTING THE STRATEGY INTO ACTION

The examples in the following lesson come from Paula Havens's fifth-grade social studies curriculum. To introduce her unit of study on fires and help students build vocabulary to discuss the Chicago Fire of 1871, Havens pairs the novel Survival! Fire *with the nonfiction text* The Great Fire. *(For more on Havens's unit, see page 22.)*

1. *Select the twin books.* Choose an engaging chapter book focused on the topic of study or theme and plan to read the book over the course of several days. Find a nonfiction text written on the topic that will encourage students to use much of the same vocabulary they will encounter in the fiction selection.

   Newspaper and magazine articles can be great sources of nonfiction text for any current-events work in social studies or science. Seek out student news magazines at your students' grade or reading level, such as *Scholastic News* and *Science World,* and check with your school librarian to see which children's periodicals he or she orders.

2. *Choose key words students need to know to comprehend the fiction text, making sure that most of the words will appear in the nonfiction text as well.* Havens chooses the following words for this lesson, including some real and fictional character names:

rebuilding	rich	1871	relief efforts	Nate	Ryan
Katherine	damage	wind	fireproof	barn	cow
insurance	Chicago	fire	Patrick	panic	O'Leary
Clark Street	firefighters	poor	Canal Street	Julie	

3. *Decide on categories or headings into which the selected words may be organized.* Havens usually uses literary elements as categories to help students anticipate the story's structure. For this lesson, she created a special activity sheet with these headings: Setting, Character, Goal/Problem, Action, Resolution, and Miscellaneous (see below). She also posts on the board a class-size Predict-O-Gram on chart paper to use during the lesson.

4. *Give each student a copy of the Predict-O-Gram sheet (page 36) that includes the list of words in the box at the top and the categories you've chosen.* Have students fill in their names and the titles of the twin books you will be using. Be sure that you explain the meanings of any category headings with which students are unfamiliar.

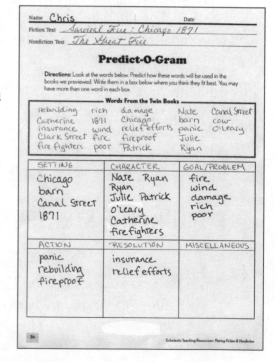

5. *Provide a brief introduction to each word so that students are able to hear and pronounce them.* Havens pronounces the words and has students repeat them but does not discuss their meanings.

6. *Pair students or have them work individually. Ask them to do their best to place each word into the appropriate category on their sheets.* After about 15 minutes, Havens signals her students to stop. Most of Havens's students choose to work with a partner; much discussing, writing, erasing, and looking perplexed ensues.

7. *Have students fill in the class Predict-O-Gram chart.* Without any discussion, Havens passes out three- by three-inch sticky-notes and asks for volunteers to choose a word from the list, write it on a note, and place it on a large Predict-O-Gram chart.

8. *Have students read (or listen to) the selected text and verify word placement.* Have students read to preselected points in the fiction book, either individually, with partners, or at home. Meanwhile, read aloud related portions of the nonfiction book. Havens reads portions of both books to the class as they follow along and encourages them to partner-read or read at home. As they come across the vocabulary words in their reading (or listening), they verify the correct placement on their own Predict-O-Gram sheets. If they discover they've placed a word in the wrong category, students use a colored pen or pencil to cross out (not erase) their original prediction and place the word in the correct category.

 After four days of listening to Havens read aloud portions of *The Great Fire*, and reading *Survival! Fire*, students complete the books and their Predict-O-Gram sheets.

9. *Revisit the Predict-O-Gram sheets to confirm or refute choices.* Havens asks for volunteers to reposition the sticky-notes on the class Predict-O-Gram into the correct categories. She discusses with students why they placed a certain word into a category originally but later changed their minds. After discussing and verifying word meanings and relationships, students remove the sticky-notes and write the word with a marker into the correct category. Students who didn't manage to get the words into the correct categories during reading may now "fix" their sheets as the class discusses the words.

10. *Have students write a story or report that uses some of their newly acquired words and information they have learned about the topic.* Havens assigns her students to write about some of what they learned from the twin books and the Predict-O-Gram lesson. Students write on a variety of topics: Grace wrote about when her Granna's house caught on fire, Matt wrote about the fire in his aunt's car, and Jared wrote about the brush fire he saw on TV.

11. *Evaluate.* Give students a target number of vocabulary words from the Predict-O-Gram that they must use accurately in their writing and assign points for each word used correctly in context. For more structured writing, you may want to create a rubric that includes a target number of vocabulary words for students to use, as well as structural and mechanical goals. Havens's students' reflective writing shows the information and vocabulary they've learned from class and current-events discussions—most were able to make references to the Chicago Fire and successfully integrate about 50 to 70 percent of the words into their narratives.

Strategy Spotlight: **PREDICT-O-GRAM**

The Twin Books:

FICTION

Survival! Fire
by Kathleen Duey and Karen A. Bale
(Aladdin, 1998)

It's Chicago, October 8, 1871. Fate brings two unlikely young people together on the chaotic streets of Chicago. Nate becomes a hero for his bravery and courage in rescuing Julie from kidnappers. This book is part of the Survival! series, in which young people survive adventures through courage and determination.

NONFICTION

The Great Fire
by Jim Murphy
(Scholastic, 1995)

In this Newbery Honor Book about the Great Fire in Chicago in 1871, authentic artwork from historical collections adds to the wealth of information gathered about the disastrous fire. It includes actual survivors' accounts taken from newspapers and other writings.

■ Classroom Context

Paula Havens's fifth graders love discussing current events, and she encourages them to read about and share with the class news that interests them. Her students look forward to reading and discussing newspaper and magazine articles from class subscriptions and from other sources she and students bring in. Whenever she can, Havens ties recent events in to her social studies and science curriculum.

One Monday morning Havens's students came in talking about a warehouse fire that had occurred three blocks from the school on Friday night. Havens read about the fire and, over the weekend, redesigned her lesson plans to tie this real-life event to several state/district goals in social studies, science, and language arts. She also located an article in her social studies textbook on the 1871 Chicago Fire. She stopped on the way to school and purchased three extra copies of the local newspaper so that her students could share in small groups.

■ Why These Twin Books?

With several literature sets from the Survival! series in the class library, Havens prepares to introduce *Survival! Fire* on Monday and have students read the book in pairs or individually. She chooses to read aloud sections of *The Great Fire* as the nonfiction book to help students see how the Chicago Fire of 1871 swept through the warehouse section of the city and influenced history. This book is a great motivator because it includes actual photographs of the Chicago Fire, and the class can compare them with newspaper pictures of the warehouse fire and with their own recent observations.

■ How the Strategy Activity Fits In

By being flexible and using twin books, Havens seamlessly integrates her social studies text's limited historical information about the Chicago Fire with an event in students' lives. After introducing the books and familiarizing the students with key words through the Predict-O-Gram, Havens sends a letter to parents about the intended study. She asks them to watch TV, to read articles and look at pictures in the newspaper, and even to drive their children by the burnt warehouse if possible. The connection to the real-life experience keeps the students' excitement high and provided more facts.

■ Success Story

Havens's students' reflective writing shows the new information and vocabulary they learned from class and at-home discussions. By using twin books and the textbook for support, Havens is able to cover a topic well in a short amount of time. Her student's writing also demonstrates that they are beginning to learn about how fires affect communities and what it means to be civic-minded.

WORD OR CONCEPT MAP
A Graphic Organizer That Teaches and Reinforces Vocabulary

OBJECTIVE

To help students prepare for reading and gain ownership of new vocabulary, and to support their comprehension.

HOW IT WORKS

Word maps help students build word-recognition skills and become more independent in acquiring new vocabulary words. Concept maps work similarly but often require students to have a broader understanding of the unit of study: These maps use an idea or theme as the main focus rather than a concrete word (for example, a concept map might focus on *human rights* while a word map might focus on *boycott*).

On both maps, the targeted word is placed in a rectangle in the center of the page. Three questions provided by Schwartz and Raphael (1985) are arranged around the word:

- What is it?

- What is it like?

- What are some examples?

Each question is set in a different shape (circle, square, or oval) that provides enough room for multiple answers. The three shapes are connected by lines to the word in the center to form a web (see the example on page 25).

WHEN TO USE WORD OR CONCEPT MAPS

■ Before Reading

Assigning a word or concept map before students read helps them focus on a key word or concept and create a frame of reference for it. Students' responses enable you to check and see how much they know about the word or concept.

■ During Reading

As students read and come upon answers to the three questions, they fill in the corresponding spaces on the maps they've created.

■ After Reading

Students review unanswered questions and search the selection again to complete the word or concept map. After answering all three questions, students should recognize and be able to use and comprehend in context the vocabulary words you've introduced with these graphic organizers.

PUTTING THE STRATEGY INTO ACTION

The examples that follow are from a human rights unit developed by fifth-grade teacher Lisa Gyger to complement material covered in her social studies textbook. By using the twin books Rosa Parks: My Story *and* A Picture of Freedom: The Diary of Clotee, a Slave Girl, *Gyger hopes to provide her students with a deep understanding of the issues explored in the books and textbook and a compelling context in which to learn related vocabulary. (For more on Gyger's unit, see page 27.)*

1. ***Select the twin books.*** Select books oriented toward the central themes or concepts of your study. Identify new vocabulary in the texts as well as key terms that may be abstract (for example, major historical concepts like freedom, slavery, independence, revolution, or human rights).

   Biographies and autobiographies are excellent nonfiction resources for this strategy. When students become engaged in one person's life story and experience the subject's struggles and triumphs, they gain insight into the global themes that story addresses. Historical fiction can serve the same purpose. The twin books should help students deepen their understanding of a concept by framing it in more than one way.

2. ***Identify several words that are essential to helping students make sense of the reading and participate in discussions.*** Choose terms that students may have heard of but may not fully understand; mapping words that require a great deal of background knowledge should be reserved for after reading, when students can connect them to real people and situations and are ready to explore them fully.

   Gyger chooses the words *prejudice, bias,* and *intolerance* for her students to use in the concept maps they complete during their reading. In her discussions with students, she makes a point of avoiding the terms *human rights* and *constitutional rights*, which she wants her students to focus on during the study but which are too broad for students to handle right now in a concept map.

3. ***Begin reading aloud or have students independently read the twin books.*** Gyger has multiple copies of the twin-book titles (a pair for each child), and she reads aloud parts of each book to introduce them. After listening, Gyger's students are eager to read aloud with partners. They partner-read several pages, agree on a good stopping point, and then discuss what they've read. (It takes several days of class and read-at-home time for students to complete both books. During this time, Gyger has students discuss the books and key terms with family members or other people who lived through the 1960s.)

4. ***Model the word-map strategy with students before they create their own maps.*** Using a transparency of page 37, fill in the map, starting with a word or concept students can easily understand, for example, *ice cream*. Use *ice cream* to explain to stu-

dents how to give useful definitions, synonyms, and examples. (Make sure students understand that a concept is abstract—that they cannot always understand it by using their five senses.)

5. ***Give each student a copy of the Word/Concept Map reproducible and introduce the focus words.*** Put, or direct students to put, one of the focus words in the rectangle. Gyger has students begin with the word *prejudice*. Later, she has them create two additional maps with the words *bias* and *intolerance*.

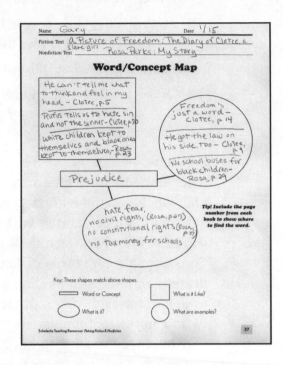

6. ***Have students ask themselves the three questions in order to understand the meaning of the focus word.***

- **What is it?** Students define the word in the oval on the map. Gyger's students use these words as part of their definition of *prejudice*: *hate, fear, no civil rights, no tax money for schools.* She writes some of these on the chart-paper diagram so everyone can see. Gyger tells students they can use some of these words when filling out their own maps, but she encourages them to select others of their own as well.

- **What is it like?** Students choose synonyms of the word to put in the square. Gyger's students use the twin books and content they've learned from discussions with classmates and family members to generate meaningful words and phrases such as *intolerance, injustice,* and *white children keeping to themselves.*

- **What are some examples?** Students offer qualities or examples of the word and write those in the circle. For *prejudice* two examples are *freedom is just a word* and *no school buses for black children.*

7. ***Discuss the completed word maps.*** You may want to discuss the maps with the whole class or have students discuss them in small groups or pairs. In this selection from Gyger's follow-up discussion with her students, she prompts students to use oral language to clarify the meaning of the word *prejudice* and to connect it to the theme of their human rights unit.

> **GYGER:** When you hear the word *prejudice*, do you think of it as a good word or a nice word?
>
> **GAREE:** Well, when somebody says, "You're prejudiced about a person's skin color," I don't think it's something I'd want someone to say about me. So, I guess it's not a nice word.

RUSS: I don't think it is either, because both the girls were not treated right in the stories.

GYGER: What do you mean by *right*?

RUSS: Well, it just seems like they were no different than any other girls but they were treated like they had something really wrong with them.

GYGER: Class, what did the white-skinned people think was wrong with them?

GRETCHEN: They just had different-colored skin. Look, I'm not the same color as Micayla, but we're still the same. They were still people and humans just like everybody else.

8. *Evaluate.*

After students have had experience both with twin books *and* with developing word and concept maps with the support of the group, give them an opportunity to create a new map independently, for homework. Use a word or concept that has not been explored fully by the group but that can be researched, if necessary, in the twin books. Consider selecting three or four words or concepts ranging from basic to more sophisticated, and allow individual students to choose one. Examine students' finished maps to determine their depth of understanding of the word or concept as well as their ability to use the mapping strategy independently.

You may also want to have students incorporate the new vocabulary they've learned in a writing project. Gyger has her students conduct interviews with adults who lived through the civil rights era. After they have collected and discussed the information from the interviews, students put together a class book about their understanding of human rights and fill it with stories and examples from the interviews. They refer to their maps as they write their stories and write out their interviews.

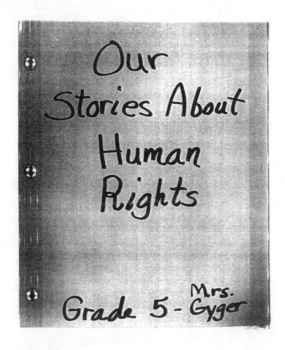

Strategy Spotlight: **WORD OR CONCEPT MAP**

The Twin Books:

FICTION

A Picture of Freedom: The Diary of Clotee, a Slave Girl
by Patricia McKissack
(Scholastic, 1997)

This Dear America series book features a slave girl, Clotee, and her efforts to gain freedom. She learns to read while fanning the plantation owner's son during his lessons. As Clotee writes in diary format, she reveals an incredible dedication to learning to read and a desire to gain freedom. She also describes how she falls in love and matures into a young woman during the tumultuous Civil War period.

NONFICTION

Rosa Parks: My Story
by Rosa Parks with Jim Haskins
(Scholastic, 1992)

Rosa Parks is forever connected to the momentous evening in Montgomery, Alabama, in 1955 when she refused to give up her bus seat to a white man. In this inspiring autobiography, Parks tells her life story and gives a personal context from which students can understand her participation in the civil rights movement.

■ Classroom Context

A fourth-grade teacher in a small, rural, but nonetheless ethnically and culturally diverse Midwestern school, Gyger continually infuses multicultural learning and respect into all her teaching. Gyger has chosen these twin books to enhance her class's yearly study of human rights. The social studies textbook she uses is fairly comprehensive, but the space it allots to the civil rights movement is limited. Twin books provide the opportunity to expand students' knowledge and understanding of the subject.

■ Why These Twin Books?

From observations she has made about students during Read Alouds and literature circles, Gyger knows that both books will build on her students' interests. These books—a diary and an autobiography—will also build on their understanding of various formats.

Also each book delivers its content in a powerful way. Clotee's diary helps provide a sense of history and culture through entries written in dialect. Rosa Parks's descriptions of how inhumanly children and adults were treated because of their skin color helps sensitize readers to the injustices that are a part of our more recent American History.

■ How the Strategy Activity Fits In:

After reading the twin books and interviewing adults who lived through the civil rights era, some students choose to revise their concept maps because they have a better understanding of the history of racial discrimination in the United States. They incorporate words they've explored in their discussions, such as *shock, horror, anger, hurt, resentment, happy, sorrow,* and *fear* into a class writing project "Our Stories About Human Rights."

■ Success Story

Reflecting upon the time she devoted to this human rights unit, Gyger sees that her students accomplished her goals and objectives for it. During class discussions, they feel comfortable taking the risk of sharing their personal feelings about their own prejudices and how their views have changed. They discuss how the main characters in the twin books are alike and how their civil rights were not upheld. They refer to their concept maps and even add additional shapes to incorporate their personal beliefs about civil rights. As she uses terms from the twin books during their writing and class discussions, Gyger notices the growth in her students' vocabulary. She sees increased ownership of the selected vocabulary words in class discussions, writing activities, and comprehension of new text material.

VOCABULARY, LANGUAGE, AND PREDICTION (VLP)

Analyze Words to Build Vocabulary and Understanding

OBJECTIVE

To help students increase word recognition and, thereby, comprehension by using word-analysis skills

HOW IT WORKS

In preparation for reading, students analyze and investigate words from the text by answering a series of questions about them. These questions, developed by the teacher, provide clues about the words' meanings and, according to researchers Wood and Robinson, "reinforce each word's structural and semantic characteristics" (1983). After answering the teacher's questions, students make predictions about the content of the text based on the vocabulary.

WHEN TO USE VOCABULARY, LANGUAGE, AND PREDICTION (VLP)

■ **Before Reading**

As a prereading strategy, VLP increases students' word recognition ability before they actually read the text. This word knowledge helps students feel confident about reading the text because they already recognize the words, know what affixes (if any) are used, understand what the words mean, and can use each one in a sentence.

PUTTING THE STRATEGY INTO ACTION

David Oliphant's fifth-grade Civil War unit provides the examples in the section that follows. Oliphant uses twin books to enhance his students' study of this tumultuous period in American history. (For more on Oliphant's unit, see page 31.)

1. *Select the twin books.* Look for books that provide a significant amount of content-area vocabulary as well as opportunities to research word meanings through text and visuals. Oliphant's students are able to use the index and glossary from *A Nation Torn* to support their reading of the novel *Thunder on the Tennessee*; the photographs in the nonfiction book also help them understand how soldiers dressed, where they slept and ate, and what the towns and cities looked like after the fierce fighting ravaged the areas.

2. **Examine the text and select the vocabulary words students need for comprehension.** Oliphant chooses the following words from *Thunder on the Tennessee*, noting the page numbers on which they appear:

Rebs	p. 8	musket	p. 35
colonel	p. 11	Federal	p. 63
regiment	p. 11	Confederate	p. 90
war	p. 12	surgeon	p. 110
slavery	p. 13	gunboats	p. 115
Yankee	p. 13	soldier	p. 115
bullets	p. 16	bayonet	p. 116
corporal	p. 33	sergeant	p. 138

3. **Determine what skills you can teach or review using the chosen words.** Oliphant's words all center on the topic of the Civil War—they are combat-related terms he wants his students to know. You may also create a narrower category, such as "weapons" (*musket, bayonet, bullets*), or have all the words be the same part of speech, such as proper nouns (*Reb, Yankee, Confederate, Federal*).

4. **Write the words on the board or on chart paper along with the page number where the word is first mentioned, but do not give any additional information about the words.** Students will use background knowledge, clues found in the questions you will ask, and the process of elimination to determine word meanings. Oliphant introduces about five words a day over three days using this method.

5. **Prepare a list of questions that will provide students with clues about word meanings and display the list on the board or on an overhead transparency.** You may want to use synonyms, antonyms, categorization, homophones, context, dictionary use, grammar, and structural analysis to create the questions. Read the questions aloud and have students answer them individually or in pairs in their notebooks. Here are some of Oliphant's questions:

- What type of physician performs operations? (*surgeon*)

- What is another name for a rifle? (*musket*)

- In the 1800s people were brought from Africa to the United States and sold to white landowners. What was this called? (*slavery*)

- Which word is a collective noun for a group of soldiers? (*regiment*)

- In which words do you find the same sound of *a* as in *play*? (*bayonet, slavery*)

After students have answered the questions, review the answers as a class to clarify any confusion students may have. Encourage them to take notes on words they missed so they can better learn word meanings. During the review, have individual students come to the board or chart and point to the word. To create a memorable focus on selected words, Oliphant has several interesting pointers—a magic wand, a flyswatter with a hole cut in the middle, a band director's baton, and several dowel rods painted bright colors. Students can select their favorite when they come to the board.

6. **Have students predict the content of the reading selection.** After you cover all the selected vocabulary words in the language phase of the lesson, have students use their knowledge of the words to predict the content of the twin-book set. Write these predictions on the board or on chart paper as the children make them.

TEACHING TIP
ADAPTING VLP FOR GROUP SIZE

Adapt the VLP strategy for small groups or individual students by writing each vocabulary word on a colorful index card rather than on the board or chart paper. When the words are lying on a table, it is easy for students to point to each word as it is described.

Your students' predictions might center on events, characterizations, setting, or mood. Oliphant focuses on all the words together to predict what the story in *Thunder on the Tennessee* is about. He encourages students to make predictions by asking: *Which words might relate to the characters in the book? Do any of these words set a mood for the story? Do these words sound like ones from a fantasy story or a realistic book? Do they sound like words you might hear on radio or television news programs?* The predictions also serve as great motivators for reading the book.

7. **Encourage students to confirm, refute, or modify their original predictions from Step 6 as they read.** Oliphant's students check the chart paper often during their reading to see how closely their predictions match the actual text. This helps them see how the vocabulary actually functions in the fiction piece, in contrast to their predictions.

8. **Evaluate.** Give students an opportunity to use the vocabulary words in a new context. For example, ask students to construct a dialogue between two characters at a crucial moment in the fictional story. Have them use vocabulary from the VLP exercise (assigning a specific number of words may be a good idea). Assess both their usage of the selected vocabulary and their understanding of the characters and story, as evidenced by the content of the dialogue.

To focus more closely on students' understanding of the word-analysis skills used in VLP, ask them to reread selections from both twin books and identify additional examples of the structural elements you have discussed in class (for example, prefixes or suffixes, parts of speech) and then list them under appropriate headings. Examine students' lists to determine how well they understand the structural elements they have researched.

Strategy Spotlight: **VOCABULARY, LANGUAGE, AND PREDICTION (VLP)**

The Twin Books:

FICTION

Thunder on the Tennessee
by G. Clifton Wisler
(Scholastic, 1983)

Fifteen-year-old Willie leaves home to join his father in the battle against the Yanks. This is a poignant story about a brave young man who discovers first-hand the realities of war.

NONFICTION

A Nation Torn: The Story of How the Civil War Began
by Delia Ray
(Scholastic, 1990)

This ALA Best Book for Young Adults portrays, in photographs and text, events leading up to the Civil War.

■ Classroom Context

Oliphant has enjoyed studying and learning about the Civil War for several years, and this enthusiasm and knowledge always carries over into his classroom. The social studies text doesn't go into enough detail for his students to truly understand the issues and historical importance of the war. Oliphant uses twin books to enhance the study. He continually emphasizes word recognition in his teaching because he knows that a well-developed vocabulary will enhance his students' comprehension.

■ Why These Twin Books?

Oliphant chooses *Thunder on the Tennessee* because its main character, Willie, is just a little older than his students, who like to identify with older kids. The book holds their interest. As students read *Thunder on the Tennessee* they can use the index and glossary from the nonfiction book, *A Nation Torn*, to check factual information they're unsure of.

And the photographs provide great visuals to help the fifth graders understand how the soldiers dressed, where they slept and ate, and what the towns and cities looked like after the fierce fighting and pillaging.

■ How The Strategy Activity Fits In

After Oliphant introduces his fifth graders to the words he selected from *Thunder on the Tennessee* by going through the VLP exercise with them, they read and discuss the book as a class. Because it contains more information than the social studies text, students refer to the nonfiction book as they each write a report about, and draw a picture of, a hero of the war. They make a display in the hallway to celebrate their study of the Civil War (see photo below). They are eager to read more about the war from the materials displayed on the table at the back of the room.

■ Success Story

Oliphant finds that his students learn new vocabulary words well and remember what they mean when they use the VLP strategy with the twin books. Their stories about the Civil War contain many of the new words. By focusing on only two books at first and content-specific vocabulary, they acquire a firm foundation on which they can build an understanding of the war. During the rest of the year they proudly refer to the words and content they've learned.

WORD STORM
A Fast-Paced Tool to Increase Content-Area Vocabulary

OBJECTIVE

To help students build content vocabulary before they encounter it in a specialized unit of study

HOW IT WORKS

Students look at the same word, in context, in both of the twin books. Then they engage in a tightly focused brainstorming activity designed to build their understanding of the word. Students integrate the new vocabulary word in several ways: They associate the word with other words or concepts, generate alternative forms of the word, speculate about its use in other contexts, identify synonyms, and use the word in a sentence (Klemp, 1994).

WHEN TO USE A WORD STORM

■ **Before Reading**

The word storm strategy is designed to focus students' attention on selected vocabulary words before they read. After completing a word storm sheet and taking notes on the word studies of their peers, students should have a working knowledge of the vocabulary words in the reading selection.

PUTTING THE STRATEGY INTO ACTION

The examples in the following section are from a presidential election unit taught by fifth-grade teacher Ed Franks. (For more on Franks's study, see page 35.)

1. ***Select the twin books.*** Choose a pair of books that share at least 15 content-area words that will build students' understanding of the topic or unit of study. Franks chooses *Woodrow, the Whitehouse Mouse* (fiction) and *The Race for President* (nonfiction).

2. ***Select words necessary for students to understand the books.*** The number of words selected depends on the age and reading level of your students. You will need to provide a page number reference for each word from both texts so that students can copy onto their word storm sheet the sentence in which their assigned word appears. At a fifth-grade level, assigning one word for every two students works well. Using the twin books, Franks puts the following list of 15 vocabulary words on chart paper for his 30 students.

president	race	candidate
vote	term	Election Day
oath	debate	inauguration
citizen	primary	Oval Office
constitution	Congress	government

3. **Divide students into pairs or small groups.** Franks's students are already paired up as literacy partners. Two students work together for a month and then change partners.

4. **Give each pair or group a copy of the Word Storm reproducible (page 38) with one chosen word written on it.** Each group should be working on a different word.

5. **Allow time for students to answer the word storm questions.** Encourage students to use dictionaries, glossaries, or other reference materials to help them answer the questions. (You may want to model how to use the references and how to share and discuss ideas with a partner.)

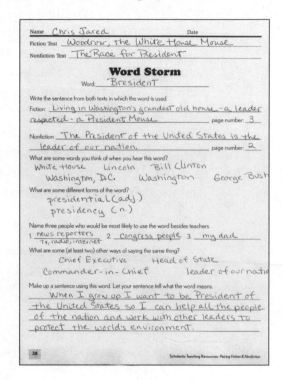

6. **Encourage students to respond creatively to enhance their comprehension.** Often, Franks's students answer all or part of the questions with artwork. He has taught this lesson successfully with crayons, paint, and paper or posterboard.

7. **Have students share their vocabulary findings.** When students have finished their word storm sheets, have the pairs "teach" the other students what their word means. Franks models creative ways of teaching a word. For example, he teaches the term *Oval Office* by first drawing an oval shape on the board. Since he knows his fifth graders respond to role-playing, he acts out a scene that describes the word. In an imaginary Oval Office, he goes to his desk, sits, straightens his tie, tries to look presidential, and pretends to phone a senator or representative.

Next he suggests that each pair spend a little time coming up with their own creative way of sharing their word knowledge rather than merely reciting answers to the word storm questions. If they choose to enact a scene, they may use a few props from the classroom collection, such as hats, pictures, campaign brochures, and buttons, or they may bring items from home. They may also share their artwork and incorporate computer graphics.

8. **Have students take notes while each group shares.** As groups report their word storm results, the rest of the class takes notes about the words under study. Franks encourages students to listen carefully and ask lots of questions during the sharing time. Students may refer to their word storm sheets to help them answer questions.

9. *Evaluate.* The "sharing" portion of this activity provides a built-in assessment tool. Teaching their peers is an ideal way for students to show what they have learned, and it is an excellent motivator as well.

As students read the twin books, remind them to watch for the vocabulary words they've studied—now they'll read them in the full context of the book. Intermittently during the study, invite pairs to review their word, explaining the context to the class and comparing the meaning in both texts. Evaluate their success in connecting their thinking and research to the context of the books—they may discover multiple meanings. Note, also, whether they are able to expand their thinking to build a definition for the word above and beyond the way in which it is used in the twin books.

As the study continues, provide students with opportunities to use the words in meaningful contexts. Franks's study culminates in a mock presidential election, for example. The class nominates presidential candidates, writes speeches, creates party platforms, counts ballots, plans the inauguration ceremony and parties, writes bills for Congress, and discusses at length several constitutional amendments. Some students choose to illustrate their favorite amendment (see below). Some even draw, to scale, the Oval Office and the exterior of the White House. In all these activities, students are using terms they've learned from their twin book readings and word-storm work.

Strategy Spotlight: **WORD STORM**

The Twin Books:

FICTION

Woodrow, the White House Mouse
by Peter W. Barnes and Cheryl Shaw Barnes
(Scholastic, 1998)

Woodrow G. Washingtail, the elected presidential candidate of the mice of the nation, takes the oath of office the same day as the people's elected presidential candidate. Woodrow takes readers on a tour of the executive mansion, explains how a bill becomes a law, and describes the role of the executive branch.

NONFICTION

The Race for President
by Leigh Hope Wood
(KidBooks, 2000)

Who is the president? How is he elected? Who gets to vote? These and other questions about the executive branch of our government are answered in simple-to-read text with brilliant pictures.

■ Classroom Context

Every year Franks teaches about elections and U.S. government. Students always feel lucky to be in his class during the presidential election year. During that year, his class has the honor of being responsible for the mock presidential election at his school. The summer before the election and early in the school year, Franks gathers many items having to do with elections, including buttons, hats, banners, news clippings, and recordings of candidates' speeches. Armed with as much information as possible, he plans lessons in all content areas to focus on the election. Early in the year he asks the art, music, and physical education teachers to help him extend this study in their own areas of expertise.

■ Why These Twin Books?

Franks adds to his collection of children's books about presidents and presidential elections almost every year. However, these twin books work especially well to begin the study during a presidential election year. *Woodrow, the White House Mouse* adds a lot of humor, and *The Race for President* is packed with information students need to know to participate effectively in the school's mock election. In addition, these twin books contain many important vocabulary words Franks knows will help his students comprehend the other reading materials he wants them to be able to use. Both are picture books, and his fifth graders enjoy the way the complicated information is presented in simple format.

■ How the Strategy Activity Fits In

Participating in the word storm activity and then reading the twin books and researching other books and materials prepares students for the culmination of this integrated unit of study—the mock election in November.

■ Success Story

Franks's students take responsibility for their assigned words because they know it's their job not only to learn their word and how to use it but also to share their knowledge with classmates. They also readily assume responsibility for taking good notes on and learning the other groups' words; they want to be ready to participate fully in the election study. Franks observes that his students frequently use their word knowledge from the twin-book work throughout this high-interest unit. A big benefit of all these activities and the twin books, which provide a tight, enjoyable focus for the beginning of the study, is that students become extremely interested in the presidential election campaign that's under way and want to understand what's happening and why it's happening. They're on the way to becoming good citizens, who vote.

Fiction Text _____

Nonfiction Text _____

Predict-O-Gram

Directions: Look at the words below. Predict how these words will be used in the books we previewed. Write them in a box below where you think they fit best. You may have more than one word in each box.

Words From the Twin Books

Name _____   Date _____

Fiction Text _____

Nonfiction Text _____

Word/Concept Map

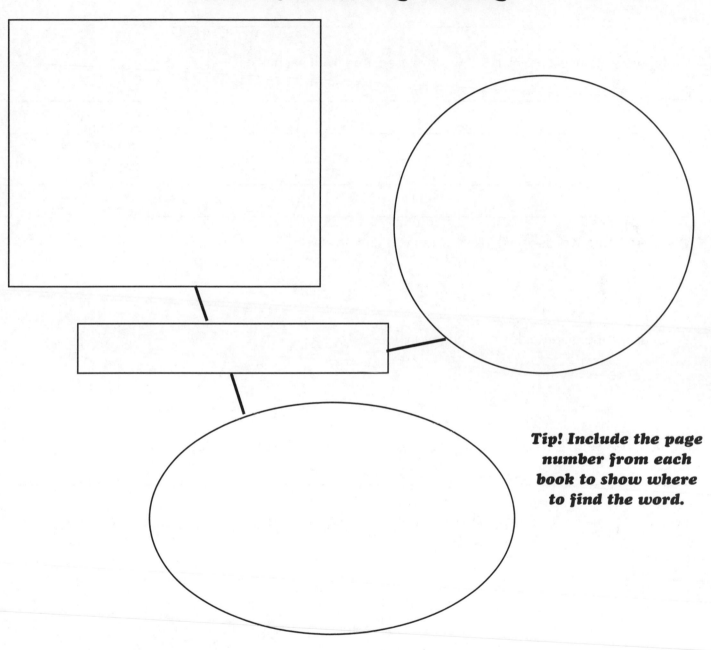

Tip! Include the page number from each book to show where to find the word.

Key: These shapes match the shapes above.

▭ Word or concept

▢ What is it like?

⬭ What is it?

◯ What are examples?

Name _____   Date _____

Fiction Text _____

Nonfiction Text _____

Word Storm

Word: _____

Write two sentences in which the word is used, one from each text.

Fiction: _____

_____ page number: _____

Nonfiction: _____

_____ page number: _____

What are some words you think of when you hear this word?

What are some different forms of the word?

Name three people who would be most likely to use the word (besides teachers).

1. _____   2. _____   3. _____

What are some (at least two) other ways of saying the same thing?

Make up a sentence using this word. Let your sentence reveal what the word means.

_____

_____

_____

_____

CHAPTER 3

Twin-Book Strategies to Enhance Reading Comprehension

Comprehension is not a set of discrete skills. Rather, it is a blend of all word recognition skills, a seamless process in which skilled reading flows from one word recognition skill to another.

—Hurst, Wilson, Camp, & Cramer, *Creating Independent Readers* (2002)

Why do we read? To understand, to learn about something that interests us. When we teach reading—especially when we're pressured by traditional reading programs and high-stakes assessments that isolate literacy skills—it's important to remember that comprehension goes beyond pronouncing words, knowing individual word meanings, or even answering simple questions about a text. It is a process of constructing meaning by interacting with the text. Good readers orchestrate a variety of skills to absorb meaning from texts, including activating prior knowledge and experiences, understanding language patterns, reflecting upon the reading selection, and having an emotional response to the selection. Good teaching helps all students learn to use comprehension strategies to read with success.

In this chapter, you'll find five strategies for teaching students to actively monitor their comprehension. Students learn to bring their own experiences into their reading, invest in their reading by making predictions and asking questions, and engage in dialogue with peers as they compare texts. The twin books provide two sources on the same topic for students to learn from and react to, which boosts students' motivation and ability to comprehend what they read.

DIRECTED READING-
(OR LISTENING-) THINKING ACTIVITY
A Prediction Strategy to Increase Comprehension

OBJECTIVE

To enhance students' comprehension by providing ways for them to think critically as they read or listen to a book read aloud

HOW IT WORKS

Teachers introduce the twin books by asking students to make predictions based on their prior knowledge of the books' subject as well as their observations about the books' titles, cover illustrations, interior illustrations, and chapter headings. As they read portions of a text aloud (Directed Listening-Thinking Activity or DL-TA) or as students read on their own (Directed Reading-Thinking Activity or DR-TA), teachers continue to ask students to predict events or the meaning of phrases and to connect pieces of information. Students revisit and revise their predictions and theories as they read further. By both establishing a clear investigative purpose for reading and encouraging students to use one twin book to enhance their understanding of the other, teachers support students in using higher-order thinking skills when listening and reading. These practices, according to Stauffer (1969), "guide [students] to take responsibility for their own learning."

WHEN TO USE DR-TA AND DL-TA

■ Before Reading

Spend time before reading to help students understand how to make logical predictions; model making careful observations about a book's cover, title, chapter titles, and so on before asking your students to do the same.

■ After Reading

After reading, have students discuss their predictions and check them for accuracy. Advise students to look back at the text material if necessary to refine and adjust their predictions based on the new information.

PUTTING THE STRATEGY INTO ACTION

The following examples describe the use of DR-TA and DL-TA in conjunction with twin books in Lynn Danica's class. Danica's fourth-grade students learn and practice critical thinking skills as they learn about Harriet Tubman's life and place in American history. (For more on Danica's unit, see page 43.)

1. **Select the twin books.** Choose twin books that encourage readers to make predictions. Look for texts with titles and cover illustrations that give clues about the content or purpose of the books. The best text choices for this strategy are those that also contain detailed, thought-provoking illustrations or photographs, maps, and other graphics. Danica plans to read aloud *Harriet and the Promised Land* (fiction) first and then follow up with *Wanted Dead or Alive* (nonfiction).

2. **Show or distribute copies of the twin books.** Begin by directing students to focus their attention on the cover of each book. Discuss details such as title, author, illustrator, cover illustrations, chapter headings, graphics, and any other particulars available.

3. **Ask questions that require students to make predictions.** For example: *What do you think this book will be about?* followed by *Why do you think that?* Accept all responses students offer (students must feel confident about offering a prediction before that skill can improve), but help them substantiate their predictions with observations about the title, illustrations, and so on. Have students write down their predictions so they can revisit them after reading.

4. **Begin with one of the twin books, setting the other aside. Read a section of text aloud, or ask students to read to a designated stopping point.** Remind them that they are looking or listening for evidence to substantiate or refute their predictions about the text.

5. **Have students revisit their predictions.** After students read the book or selection or listen to you read it, ask them to revisit their predictions to see whether they were accurate. Have students find a sentence or two to support their predictions and read them aloud. When students finish the first section of *Wanted Dead or Alive*, Danica asks about their predictions: *Is what happened what you thought would happen? Do your predictions need adjustment?* In a class discussion, Gracie volunteers that she predicted that Harriet

MAKING THOUGHTFUL PREDICTIONS

- **Use predictions to establish a purpose for reading.** Prompt students to read to find out whether their predictions are correct; in doing so, students are motivated to read using their own stated purpose. An initial purpose both you and your students may set is, *How is the information about Harriet Tubman's work in the Underground Railroad the same in the twin books? How is it different?* Purposes on a more challenging level may be, *Read to find out why Harriet became a Moses to her people* or *Read to find out how she knew where to send the slaves in the North.* Ultimately, you are helping students to start establishing their own purposes for reading.

- **Define words.** Define any unfamiliar words in the title for students if cover illustrations are not helpful for predictions. Remind students of familiar word-attack strategies, so they can read as independently as possible.

- **Use prior knowledge about the topic.** Ask students to search their prior knowledge to help them make predictions. If they have little experience with the topic, you'll have to build background on it for them to predict with any accuracy.

was running from something because she was scared. However, by reading she has discovered that Harriet was running from someone, not something—and that Harriet helped other people run away.

6. ***Continue the process.*** Have students generate new predictions on the basis of what they've learned, using prompt questions such as *What do you think is going to happen now? What are the clues to make you think that way?* Establish a new stopping point, and continue reading to test the new set of predictions. Danica asks her students, *What does that Chapter Three title, "Follow the North Star," have to do with being wanted dead or alive? Up to this point in our reading, Harriet has tried to escape many times—how do you think she might try, or plan, to escape the harsh life on the plantation again?* The questions build anticipation for continuing the reading selection. As you read aloud or students read silently to another point in the book, ask similar questions. When students are familiar with the steps of this strategy, don't require them to stop so frequently; fewer interruptions will support fluent, more focused reading.

7. ***Use the knowledge base established by reading one twin book to enhance comprehension of the other, as well as any related textbook material.*** Students will be able to make even better, more sophisticated predictions about the second text after reading the first. Well-matched twin books will complement each other as well as the textbook material they may support. For instance, a nonfiction text may supply us with a complete biographical outline and a textbook may explain salient concepts, while a historical fiction text (or even a book of poetry, as in this classroom example) will provide a sense of key characters' personalities and the drama of the story. Students can bring the same investigative, purposeful approach to all the reading they do on the topic.

8. ***Evaluate.*** When students have read both books as well as any related textbook material, evaluate their ability to read for information as well as their understanding of how to synthesize information from multiple sources. Ask them to answer a question—one that requires some critical thinking. They should use evidence from at least two different text sources to support their answer. Have them begin by writing a predicted answer based on a prereading evaluation of the texts. After reading, have them write a revised answer that draws from information they've learned from both texts.

Strategy Spotlight: **DIRECTED READING- (OR LISTENING-) THINKING ACTIVITY**

The Twin Books:

FICTION

Harriet and the Promised Land
by Jacob Lawrence
(Aladdin, 1997)

The story of Harriet Tubman's work as a conductor on the Underground Railroad is shared through lyrical poetry and brilliant paintings that reflect the humanity of her actions, the importance of freedom, and the danger of the situation.

NONFICTION

Wanted Dead or Alive: The True Story of Harriet Tubman
by Ann McGovern
(Scholastic, 1965)

This easy-to-read chapter book gives factual information about Harriet Tubman's life and how she led hundreds of people to freedom on the Underground Railroad.

■ Classroom Context

Danica introduces her students to a wide range of literature from many genres, weaving word identification and comprehension skills into her lessons. She wants her students to be critical thinkers, questioners, and information seekers. She also wants them to develop respect for diversity in all aspects—skin color, physical attributes, ethnic groups, and economic levels. Expanding on the information contained in her social studies textbook, Danica uses twin books to study Harriet Tubman's life in greater depth, and in so doing creates opportunities to bring together much of what she values as a teacher.

■ Why These Twin Books?

Danica often pairs a book of poetry with a nonfiction book. Reading poetry allows her students to develop an appreciation for rhythm and unconventional uses of language, while adding emotional depth to content.

The nonfiction selection Danica has chosen, *Wanted Dead or Alive*, supplies the depth of information her students need to make sense of Harriet Tubman's place in history and to better comprehend their social studies book. Both books have compelling titles and cover illustrations, inspiring students to make predictions that they want to test as they read on—a great way to introduce DR-TA.

■ How the Strategy Activity Fits In

This lesson is one of several throughout the year that focuses on critical thinking. Because of the required state assessments for fourth graders, it is important that Danica's students be able to read and analyze a piece of text. DR-TA will be one of the tools students can use as they approach reading passages; Danica will continue to remind students to make initial predictions and check those predictions as they read to formulate a personal learning statement about the text or texts.

■ Success Story

After several lessons in which she pairs the DR-TA/DL-TA strategy with twin books, Danica is pleased to see dramatic improvement in her students' ability to comprehend text on a higher level. The process of making thoughtful predictions leads to purposeful, focused reading, and the purposeful reading of one text, in turn, enhances students' understanding of the other. Danica's students' learning is reflected in their contributions to class discussions, in their writing, and in consistently high achievement test scores.

K-W-L (KNOW-WANT TO KNOW-LEARNED)

Activating Prior Knowledge to Read With Purpose

OBJECTIVE

To integrate students' prior knowledge of a topic into a study so that they are eager to understand and retain key concepts and information

HOW IT WORKS

The K-W-L strategy helps students organize information, based on what they know about a topic (K), what they want to know (W), and what they have learned by reading (L). The work is done in a simple three-column chart, as shown in the example on page 47. Literacy expert Donna Ogle, who developed the strategy, explains that the K-W-L method "helps teachers become more responsive to students' knowledge and interests when reading. . . . It models for students the active thinking involved in reading" (1986).

WHEN TO USE K-W-L

■ Before Reading

Listing what they already know about a topic (K) focuses students' attention on the topic by activating prior knowledge or uncovering misconceptions. As shown in the classroom example, this segment may actually be completed *between* the reading of the fiction book and the nonfiction book in the twin-book set.

■ After Reading

After reading, students check their K and W (what I want to know) columns to determine whether what they thought they knew is accurate and to find out whether their questions have been answered from the reading. Because the earlier steps have aroused their curiosity, students are likely to retain what they have learned.

PUTTING THE STRATEGY INTO ACTION

The examples in this chapter are taken from a second/third-grade unit on nocturnal animals taught by Vista Stout. In this segment of the unit, Stout's students are learning about bats, using the twin books Stellaluna *and* Bats. *(For more on Stout's unit, see page 48.)*

1. *Select the twin books.* The fiction text you select for this twin-book set should inspire questions that can be answered by reading the nonfiction text. Take care to select a fiction book that will not confuse your students by reinforcing their misconceptions about a topic or presenting a story in an unrealistic setting. The nonfiction text you choose as a companion need not necessarily be read cover to cover by your students. With that in mind, select a nonfiction book with a full table of contents and index, so that students can research answers to their questions independently. Make additional nonfiction resources on the topic available in the classroom so that students can pursue answers to questions not answered in the primary nonfiction selection.

2. *Choose a topic for the K-W-L chart.* Find a word or phrase related to your lesson or unit of study that will elicit a lot of interest and generate thoughtful questions. Avoid selecting a topic that is too broad. If, for example, the topic "nocturnal animals" results in responses that are too vague to guide students' research in the nonfiction text, consider choosing a more specific topic, such as bats.

3. *Introduce or read aloud the fiction book before you work with the K-W-L chart.* Have students read the fiction selection or read it aloud to them to stimulate their interest in the topic and help build background knowledge. Stout reads *Stellaluna* to her class at this point. In fact, she reads it twice—once without discussion and then again, encouraging comments and discussion about Stellaluna's character and habits and the details of the illustrations.

4. *Prepare the K-W-L graphic organizer.* Either distribute copies of the K-W-L Chart reproducible on page 64 or have students divide a page in thirds and label the left column *K*, the middle column *W*, and the right column *L*. (You may also want to create a large version on chart paper, on the chalkboard, or on an overhead.) Identify the topic and be sure that students understand what the *K*, *W*, and *L* stand for.

5. *Ask students what they already know about the topic.* Conduct a brainstorming session in which you record all ideas students generate about the topic. Encourage students to use their prior knowledge, including what they learned from the fiction selection. Record ideas in the K column on chart paper or the chalkboard or have students write the ideas down on their copies of the K-W-L chart. If students are working individually or in pairs, follow up by consolidating their ideas onto a class version of the K-W-L chart. This activity will show you what students know or believe they know about the topic. Resist the urge to correct ideas or teach content at this point; there will be an opportunity later in the process to discover and correct misconceptions.

6. *Find out what students want to know about the topic.* As they fill in the second part of the graphic organizer, students develop a purpose for reading by articulating what

they want to know. Students may complete this step individually, in groups, or as a class. You may lead a class discussion by asking students questions based on their responses in the K category and, if appropriate, by drawing attention to issues in the fiction selection. Add these questions to the W column of the chart.

After a few minutes of discussion, Stout's students are able to form questions about what they want to know about nocturnal animals, and bats in particular. Questions include *How do nocturnal animals see at night? Why don't they fly into things? What do real bats eat? What kind of bat was Stellaluna? What colors are bats? Why are bats so ugly? What sounds do bats make? How big are most bats? Where do bats live?* Stout modifies some questions for the purposes of clarity, then adds them to the class chart (see photo on the next page).

7. **Have students research the answers to their questions in the nonfiction text.** As students read or listen to you read the nonfiction book, remind them to remain focused on the questions they generated in the previous step. You may consider asking students to pause periodically and record their findings in the L (what we learned) column of the graphic organizer.

TEACHING TIP

VARYING THE K-W-L FORMAT

There are several variations you can try with the original K-W-L. K-W-L-A adds an **Answer** column, where students list sources that they plan to use to find answers to the questions they wrote in the W column. Another variation, K-W-L-E, includes an **Effect** column, in which students describe how they responded to the selection. A third version, K-W-L-S, provides a **Still Want to Know** column, in which students write unanswered questions. These more advanced variations help students either think about their process for learning information from their reading (K-W-L-A), reflect on what they've learned (K-W-L-E), and set goals for ongoing study and (K-W-L-S).

8. **After students have read or listened to both texts, ask them what they have learned.** Referring students to the questions they generated for the W column on the chart, ask them to explain what they learned from the texts. Write the answers to students' questions in the L column on the chart or have students write them on their individual sheets.

Stout's students ask her to reread parts of *Bats* to help them answer specific questions. She writes unanswered questions from students' charts on the chart paper and keeps this list available for students to answer at another time, after further reading. Be sure to have additional resources for research available in the classroom so that students have the opportunity to satisfy their curiosity.

9. *Evaluate.* You need to monitor each step of the K-W-L process to evaluate its success with your students. To glean factual information from the fiction text, students may have to infer and generalize. To formulate questions, they need to think critically about the topic. To search efficiently for the answers to their questions in the nonfiction text, they probably need to use the index and table of contents of the book and then scan for relevant information.

In addition, students should be able to reconsider their prior knowledge about a topic, identify and correct misconceptions, and explain how they discovered those misconceptions.

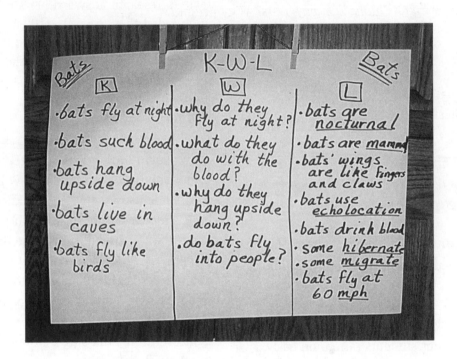

Strategy Spotlight: **K·W·L**

The Twin Books:

FICTION

Stellaluna
by Janell Cannon
(Harcourt Brace, 1993)

Stellaluna, a baby bat separated from her mother, discovers that all animals that fly are not like her. For example, they have different eating preferences and sleeping habits. She learns to adjust to her environment and makes friends along the way.

NONFICTION

Bats
by Celia Bland
(Scholastic, 1996)

The close-up photographs and informative narrative tell the reader all about bats. This fact-filled book covers such topics as where bats live, how they see at night, and their predatory habits.

■ Classroom Context

As part of an integrated unit on nocturnal animals, Stout chooses twin books along with the K-W-L strategy to help her second- and third-grade students learn about bats. Experience has taught her the value of capturing her students' attention early when she begins a new study; introducing her students to compelling fiction and activating their prior knowledge through the K-W-L strategy is an effective way to engage their imaginations and generate interest in the topic.

■ Why These Twin Books?

An important element of teaching comprehension is to activate students' prior knowledge. Stout often uses the fiction book of a twin-book set to focus her students' attention on what they already know about a topic—in this case, bats. *Stellaluna* does so very effectively. Since her students usually have mis-

conceptions about bats, Stout chooses the nonfiction book *Bats* to address these. The children appreciate the happy ending of *Stellaluna* and the close-up pictures in *Bats*.

■ How the Strategy Fits In

This unit of nocturnal animals is part of a larger unit of study on mammals. Stout continues to use twin books in conjunction with K-W-L as students learn about other mammals. By repeating the process of activating prior knowledge, generating questions, and using information gathered from two texts to research answers, her students are able to apply what they learn from their specific study of bats and, later, other animals to the larger picture of understanding habitats, life cycles, behaviors, and other characteristics of nocturnal animals.

■ Success Story

Stout has found that the K-W-L chart is a perfect complement to the twin-book technique she uses throughout her lessons. The K-W-L strategy encourages students to activate prior knowledge about the topic, to concentrate on what they want to know about the topic, and to measure their own understanding after reading. Using twin books allows students to research the answers to their own questions in a new text. Her students remain engaged in the study while monitoring their own reading comprehension through all stages of reading—from prereading through reflection.

LITERATURE CIRCLES
Enhancing Reading Response Skills Through
Peer Discussions

OBJECTIVE

To enhance students' comprehension and enjoyment of literature by providing a structured context in which to respond to it—through discussions with their peers

HOW IT WORKS

Students are organized into literature circles, small groups that meet at regularly scheduled times. Students within each literature circle read the same book, progress at the same pace, and use their meeting time to discuss or do projects focused on what they've read. Teachers may assign students specific roles in the group discussion or allow children to discuss their reading in a less structured way.

Students grouped in literature circles may read one of the twin books (some groups read the fiction book while others read the nonfiction book) or read both books in a different order (some groups read the fiction book first and the nonfiction book second, while others read the books in the reverse order). Members of each literature circle have opportunities to share learning and understanding with the other circles, which enriches everyone's experience.

Teachers actively model ways to engage in productive discussions about literature, taking a bigger part in group discussion at first and gradually stepping back to let students control the talk. Ultimately, as Harris and Hodges (1995) point out, literature circles provide students with a valuable opportunity to discuss books independently of the teacher.

WHEN TO USE LITERATURE CIRCLES

■ During Reading

Groups set goals for completing their reading and also for focusing their discussions. They meet regularly until they have completed the book.

■ After Reading

Closure to book discussions, in which groups share their learning with the class, can take several forms, as described in Step 9 below,.

PUTTING THE STRATEGY INTO ACTION

The examples in this chapter are drawn from a fifth-grade unit on the Holocaust taught by Kenneth Roseman. Using twin books Anna Is Still Here *and* A Place to Hide: True Stories of Holocaust Rescues, *Roseman provides his students with rich information about the topic. (For more on Roseman's unit, see page 53.)*

1. ***Decide how you will group your students.*** The structure of literature circles is flexible and can be tailored to the needs of your class. Choose a grouping strategy first, because it may affect your text selections.

You may want to allow students to group themselves by asking them to join with others who plan to read the same book, or you can organize the groups yourself and assign each group a book. You may also choose to group students by reading level or create mixed-ability groups. Throughout the course of a unit, let the groups remain intact while books rotate, so that each group reads two books together.

Make sure groups are large enough to encourage a good discussion, yet small enough to require every member's participation; three to five students per group usually works well for grades 3–5. Groups with older or more mature readers may be larger and may work together without teacher assistance for longer periods at a time than those with younger or less mature readers.

Roseman plans to group students into literature circles of four, based on their book choices, personalities, and reading abilities.

2. ***Determine how many titles to offer students and select the books.*** Once you know how many groups of students you will have, decide how many books to offer. Depending on the time you have to devote to a study, you may choose to offer your students between two and five different titles (more than five choices may become very difficult to manage). In this study, Roseman offers students a fiction and a nonfiction book on Holocaust rescue missions. At the end of the study, he wants students to share and compare the information they've absorbed from both books.

3. ***Introduce the text selections with short "commercials" or book talks.*** If students will be choosing their own books, these book talks will help them make informed choices; if you plan to assign books to your students, the book talks will reinforce the idea that the whole class is gathering knowledge about a topic by using multiple sources.

Roseman presents brief book commercials for both of the twin books. He explains that in the fiction book, Anna, a Jewish girl, survives the war but struggles to cope with her postwar life in the Netherlands. He points out that the nonfiction book contains brief biographies of Holocaust heroes who were instrumental in saving and rescuing many Jewish people. Roseman then asks students to choose which of the two books they want to read first. With multiple copies of each book, he is able to assign most students their first choice.

4. **Group students and either designate a job for each group member or encourage open-ended discussions.** After students complete a voting ballot, Roseman creates groups of four. You may choose to assign a specific job to each group member and have students rotate through the jobs during the book study. Specific jobs may include discussion leader, illustrator, and language researcher to look up and record troublesome or interesting words. Or you may choose, as Roseman does with this lesson, to assign only a group leader and let the discussion flow more naturally. Either way, be sure you model good group discussion techniques including questioning, listening, behaving respectfully, and responding within a group.

5. **Choose meeting times.** Establish dates and times for literature circles to meet. You may want the groups to meet daily or every other day, keeping in mind that students need in-class time to read and reflect on the text. Letting too much time elapse between meetings will make it difficult for students to stay invested in their reading. For older students or more mature readers, some reading may be assigned as homework so that more class time is available for the literature-circle discussion.

   Roseman decides to use his scheduled reading-instruction time of 50 minutes for literature circles on Mondays, Wednesdays, and Fridays. He anticipates that this unit will last about three weeks—perhaps longer if students show a keen interest. He also anticipates that he'll use some of the scheduled social studies time for his students to read the twin books.

6. **Hold an initial meeting to launch the literature group process.** Roseman begins literature-circle time with these twin books by meeting with the three groups that chose the fiction book. He reads aloud the first 11 pages, stopping at the point where Anna is ridiculed for not being in the same grade at school as other children her age. A brief discussion immediately ensues about how his students might feel in the same situation; Roseman guides students to listen carefully to each speaker and offer thoughtful responses. At the end of the discussion, he asks the three groups to read through page 23 by Friday and have at least three comments and or questions written in their literature-circle response journals about what they have read.

   During independent reading time, Roseman meets with the three groups who chose the nonfiction book about Holocaust heroes. He reads aloud the acknowledgments, foreword, and introduction, to help students understand how the heroes were chosen for the book. Students turn to the center of the book, where photos are displayed. Following a discussion, Roseman asks students to read the first chapter, about Miep, by Friday and write at least three comments and/or questions in their journals about how 24-year-old Miep became a hero to Jews in Amsterdam.

7. **Launch the first independent discussion, taking an active role in the literature circles to help students meet their goals.** On Friday, Roseman asks students to move into their literature circles to begin discussing their reading assignment. He asks a designated group leader to begin the discussion with leading questions, such as *What is*

the book (or chapter) about? and What is your favorite part of the book (or chapter) and why? Roseman quickly moves from group to group to make certain they understand what they are to do. After that, he joins each group as a participant, providing feedback and sharing his own comments with students in order to facilitate the discussion. Following his lead from the original assignment, each group decides how much they'll read for the following Monday.

8. **Hold as many follow-up literature-circle meetings as are needed for students to complete their reading. Make a habit of circulating among the groups and evaluating the quality of their discussions.** As literature circles continue to meet to discuss the books, monitor each group carefully to determine whether students are on task and understand the procedure. Monitoring may consist of observing each group and taking notes or completing a checklist like the Literature Circle Discussion Skills reproducible on page 65.

Roseman uses completed evaluations like the one shown here to give specific feedback and guidance as the groups set goals and lead discussions over the course of reading the books. Through modeling and participating in each group, he helps students to engage actively in the discussions.

Literature Circle Discussion Skills

Book Title: _Anna Is Still Here_   Date _2/15_
Pages/Chapters Assigned: _pp 7-16_   Book's Reading Level _5_

Group members	On task	Takes part in discussion	Listens when others speak	Read assignment	Specific job
Brian	2	1	1	2	—
Zach	1	2	2	2	—
Melissa	1	1	1	2	—
Stacie	1	2 seems apprehensive	1	2 not sure she read it	—

Overall comments about group: _All are doing well. Zach seems to be carrying most of the discussion. I'll spend more time with this group on Thursday._

1 = outstanding
2 = good
3 = needs improvement

Scholastic Teaching Resources: Pairing Fiction & Nonfiction   65

9. **Have literature circles participate in an end-of-unit share about the books and the topic of study.** At the conclusion of the book study, encourage groups to share information they learned from their work in literature circles. Students who have read the nonfiction text can provide historical context for students who read the fiction book; in turn, students who have read the fiction book can offer their peers the more personal, in-depth understanding of events described in the nonfiction text.

In addition to sharing with their classmates through class discussion, students may stage parts of the books, create displays of artwork, or present written reports.

10. **Evaluate.** When all students have had experience with at least two texts—either by reading both in their literature circles or by reading one and participating in whole-class discussions on other books on the same topic—give them a writing assignment that asks them to synthesize information from two sources. For instance, Roseman asks students to select the story of a heroic rescuer from the nonfiction book and imagine, based on their understanding of Anna's story, how their experience during the war may affect their lives afterward.

Strategy Spotlight: **LITERATURE CIRCLES**

The Twin Books:

FICTION

Anna Is Still Here
by Ida Vos
(Scholastic, 1986)

Fourteen-year-old Anna Markus hid for three years in her neighbor's attic during World War II. Now that the war is over, she still has many fears related to the past. Worst of all is that her parents refuse to discuss the war and those three lost years.

NONFICTION

A Place to Hide: True Stories of Holocaust Rescues
by Jayne Pettit
(Scholastic, 1993)

Between the years of 1933 and 1945, six million Jews were murdered. This is a collection of stories about brave people who risked their own lives to help the Jews.

■ Classroom Context

One of Roseman's top priorities is to share with his students information about diverse cultures. Roseman's basal series, which contains a short piece about Anne Frank, elicits many questions about Jewish culture (which is unfamiliar to many of his students). The basal series and social studies textbook touch on many issues of diversity, but because of limited space the content lacks depth. So Roseman decides to teach his Holocaust lessons using the basal reading piece, information from the social studies textbook, his own Jewish family history, and the twin books with literature circles. This approach allows his students to learn more about Jewish culture and world history and incorporates several district and state curricular goals.

■ Why These Twin Books?

The Holocaust and its historical context are difficult for many American students to comprehend. By selecting a fiction text with a heroine just a few years older than his students, Roseman has given his students a way to relate personally to a story far beyond their personal experience. His nonfiction text, which focuses on true stories of bravery in extreme circumstances, captivates his young readers and helps them better understand the scope of destruction and terror during this wartime era.

■ How the Strategy Fits In

Roseman begins his study of the Holocaust by having his students partner-read the general information offered in the fifth-grade social studies textbook. They also read a short biography about Anne Frank in their basal reader. Roseman enlivens their discussions with stories and artifacts of his own family history. After this introduction, Roseman starts the literature-circles lesson with the twin books.

■ Success Story

Roseman is pleased with his students' growing ability to read critically and constructively respond to literature in a discussion format. He notes that when he introduced his students to literature circles, they almost exclusively asked questions that could be answered with a yes or no or by briefly consulting the text. After about five months of working in literature circles, his students ask questions that call for higher-level thinking such as evaluating and synthesizing book information and that bring their own background knowledge into the group discussion. Moreover, the interactions among students in their literature circles provide practice with the kinds of discussions people outside classrooms have every day, and they are excellent training for working within a group situation.

READ (READ, EXAMINE, ANTICIPATE, DEVELOP)

Focusing on Meaning While Building Vocabulary

OBJECTIVE

To increase students' ability to comprehend a text and to help them build a solid vocabulary base prior to their reading

HOW IT WORKS

READ is an easy-to-remember strategy: R—read the title, E—examine vocabulary words and illustrations, A—anticipate the type of text structure used, and D—develop the importance of prior knowledge (Camp, 2001).

Using this strategy encourages students to think in a variety of ways about the book they will read: by noting its title, illustrations, and structure; noticing and integrating new vocabulary as they read; and connecting new information to what they already know. In combination, these practices help students approach a new text in a focused way, make sense of what they read, and retain new vocabulary.

WHEN TO USE READ

■ **Before Reading**

This four-step prereading process will set students up for success in reading and understanding any text. Once students are familiar with the steps, the activity won't take very long. However, when you introduce the strategy you'll probably want to devote lesson time to modeling each READ step.

PUTTING THE STRATEGY INTO ACTION

The examples that follow are taken from Exploring America, *a third-grade social studies unit taught by Stacie Stapleton. Stapleton uses twin books* The Long Way to a New Land *and* Coming to America: The Story of Immigration *to develop and deepen her students' understanding of themes in her social studies textbook. (For more on Stapleton's unit, see pages 57–58.)*

1. ***Select the twin books.*** Choose twin books that will build upon your students' current understanding of a topic. While the books you choose should be accessible to your students, they should also contain ideas and vocabulary that are new to them. Look for books that have illustrations and/or photographs that will offer students additional

(and, of course, accurate) information about the topic of study. Finally, try to find books with contrasting formats and structures (see Step 4).

2. *Model the READ strategy.*

    a. Read the title. Students often approach a book without giving much thought to the information included on the book cover. Carefully considering the title encourages students to focus on the purpose or content of a book.

        Stapleton first reads aloud to her class *Coming to America: The Story of Immigration*, the nonfiction twin book, modeling the READ strategy. She begins by asking students to consider the title. Students have a chance to ask questions about the title and discuss their interpretations. Next, Stapleton asks students to focus on the cover illustration. Students recognize the Statue of Liberty and notice that people of all ages and cultures appear to be happily waving to the statue.

    b. Examine vocabulary words and illustrations. Thumb through the book with your students, stopping every few pages on illustrations and unfamiliar words. Students will quickly get a feel for the book. This is the time to preteach vocabulary words and discuss visuals such as illustrations, charts, and graphs. Stapleton holds the book up for the whole class to see as she thumbs through it several times, stopping to point out relevant material. On chart paper, she writes the vocabulary words *Native Americans*, *descendants*, *civilizations*, *European*, *Swiss*, *Scotch-Irish*, *Ellis Island*, *refugees*, and *melting pot* as she comes across them. She leaves space to add more words later.

        Stapleton also invites a brief discussion about several illustrations but reserves most for discussion later, after they have read the book. This "thumb-through— stop" procedure builds anticipation for reading and understanding the selection and helps students develop questions to guide them through the text.

    c. Anticipate the text structure. If your students are not already familiar with a variety of text structures and formats, take a few minutes to provide some examples. Stapleton explains that nonfiction books may be structured in different ways, such as compare-and-contrast and question-and-answer formats, or with events related in chronological order (often spanning a long period in history); fiction books may be arranged in chapters, written from a single point of view or multiple points of view, or presented as a series of letters written by the book's characters. Stapleton points out that the nonfiction book *Coming to America* is written in chronological order and that hundreds of years of history are described in very few pages.

    d. Develop prior knowledge. This last step in the READ process is essential to every lesson. Students who can connect the books' topics with their own knowledge have definite advantages over those who can't. If you find that students have no prior knowledge about the topic, you'll have to build background that will enable them to comprehend the text. Stapleton helps her students make connections between the text they are about to read, what they learned in earlier grades about early explorers of North America, and what they have already read about immigration in their social studies textbook.

3. *Have students read the first twin book independently, or read it aloud.* Stapleton reads aloud to her class *The Long Way to a New Land*. As she reads, she and her students add several words and terms to the list of vocabulary words and examine the words in the context of the reading.

4. *Ask students to repeat the READ strategy with the other twin book.* Now that her students have quite a bit of knowledge about how North America was settled, Stapleton shares the nonfiction book, *Coming to America*. She has enough copies for students to work in pairs. Again, she uses the READ strategy to aid their comprehension. She reviews the purpose of using READ, what each letter represents, and how the strategy can help them understand what they're going to read.

    Stapleton gives partners about 15 minutes to go through the READ strategy with this book. She walks around the classroom, quietly encouraging each pair to read the title and look closely at the cover illustrations. She reminds students to do a thumb-through—stop of the book, examining key vocabulary words and writing down some words they don't understand or want to discuss further. Stapleton's students note that the book contains maps, illustrations of people and items such as clothing and tools, and pictures of artists' paintings. They also discover mini-biographies of explorers along with an index on the inside back cover. Next, Stapleton reminds students to anticipate the text structure. They find that the text structure is a time line of the exploration of North America, organized from earliest to latest by the dates of key journeys and events. Finally, Stapleton prompts partners to discuss their prior knowledge—what they already know about time periods included in the book.

5. *Evaluate.* Create an assignment that requires students to demonstrate their understanding of new vocabulary *and* link their learning to prior knowledge of the topic. A careful and accurate illustration of an important object, scene, idea, or relationship explored in the study, accompanied by labels or text, is an excellent way to bring these elements together. The students in Stapleton's class create labeled drawings of sailing ships, linking their new knowledge of how immigrants reached America with their prior knowledge of earlier explorers and using a variety of new words in the process.

Strategy Spotlight: **READ**

The Twin Books:

FICTION

The Long Way to a New Land
by Joan Sandis
(Sagebrush Educational Resources, 1986)

A family is driven by hunger from their home in Sweden to find a better life in America. Many hardships await the family on their journey by both sea and land.

NONFICTION

Coming to America: The Story of Immigration
by Betsy Maestro
(Scholastic, 1996)

The United States is home to people of many cultures. This book follows the story of immigration from the time before European settlement to the diverse population of today's United States. Many reasons for why people leave their homelands and come to America are explored.

■ Classroom Context

To meet educational standards, Stapleton's third graders are expected to compare and contrast differing historical accounts of United States history and understand why those events are important in today's culture. Stapleton chooses twin books to extend the information in the social studies textbook, pairing a fiction and a nonfiction book about immigration to the United States.

■ Why These Twin books?

Stapleton frequently uses children's literature to bridge the gap between what children already know from the previous year and what she wants them to know at the end of the current school year. From

previous grades, her students have a basic understanding of the European exploration of the New World; they also have read an overview of United States immigration history in their social studies textbooks.

Reading *Coming to America* broadens and deepens her students' understanding of immigration as a concept and helps them understand the diversity of the immigrant experience in America. This nonfiction text also serves as a reference to help students answer questions they have about immigration. Reading the fiction book *The Long Way to a New Land* provides a narrower but more detailed picture of immigration—Stapleton's students get a close-up view of one family's experience of leaving their home country and building a new life in the United States.

■ How the Strategy Fits In

This lesson is part of a larger unit on exploration, specifically the exploration and settling of America. Stapleton uses other twin books with the READ strategy to study other aspects of the Exploring America unit:

FICTION: *Around the World in a Hundred Years* by Jean Fritz (Penguin Putnam, 1994)

NONFICTION: *Magellan: A Voyage Around the World* by Fiona MacDonald (Franklin Watts, 1998)

•

FICTION: *Explorers Who Got Lost* by Diane Sansevere-Dreher (1992, Tor Books)

NONFICTION: *The Discovery of the Americas* by Betsy and Giulio Maestro (1992, HarperTrophy)

■ Success Story

Stapleton finds that using the READ strategy with twin books is an effective way to meet grade-level objectives in social studies. Students have a good overview of what's coming, and they can combine and improve skills that make what they read interesting and meaningful, while accumulating new content-area vocabulary.

Stapleton's students demonstrate their new understanding in two culminating projects. Since they have been particularly fascinated with sailing ships throughout the exploration and immigration study, Stapleton asks them to draw information from the various texts read by the class to create detailed, labeled drawings of period sailing ships (see photo below). The finished projects demonstrate a command of new vocabulary encountered in the study as well as the students' ability to synthesize information from multiple sources.

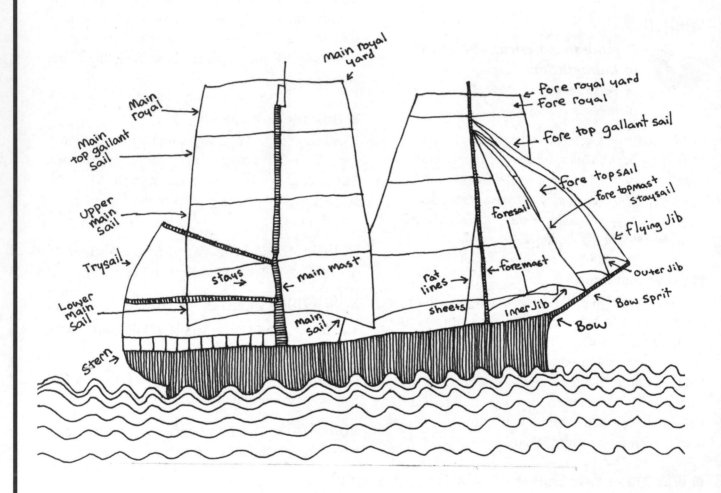

ReQUEST
Questioning to Develop Critical Thinking

OBJECTIVE

To enable students to better analyze a text and improve their understanding of the material presented in the text

HOW IT WORKS

ReQuest ("reciprocal questioning") is a procedure that provides students with guided practice in developing purposeful questions about their reading. Teachers using the ReQuest procedure help students learn to recognize and formulate questions that require critical thinking to answer. By "providing an active learning situation for the development of questioning behaviors," ReQuest markedly improves comprehension while encouraging students to become active participants in the reading process (Manzo, 1969).

WHEN TO USE ReQUEST

■ Before Reading

Prior to reading, be sure students understand that there are different types of questions readers can ask about what they read: literal, text-based questions and those that require higher-order thinking and reasoning (for example, drawing on prior knowledge and experience, making personal connections to text, and making connections between texts).

■ During Reading

Invite students to ask questions based on the content of what they've read so far. Answer their questions, and in doing so model your methods for finding or supporting the answers (see Step 6). Encourage them to make predictions about what will come next or what they will learn about next.

■ After Reading

Discuss the kinds of questions students asked and the responses they yielded. Follow up with questioning activities focused on new vocabulary found in the selection.

PUTTING THE STRATEGY INTO ACTION

The following examples are drawn from a fourth-grade westward expansion unit, the final segment of which is focused on the lives of pioneer children. Teacher Lee Davin uses twin books West to a Land of Plenty: The Diary of Teresa Angelino Viscardi *and* Children of the Wild West *to help his students develop a more personal connection to this time in history. (For more on Davin's unit, see pages 62–63.)*

1. ***Choose the twin books.*** The twin books you read using the ReQuest strategy should introduce students to new vocabulary and unfamiliar concepts, yet be accessible enough to facilitate independent reading. Remember that one of the goals of ReQuest is that students will formulate questions requiring higher-order critical thinking. Be sure that both the fiction and nonfiction selections have enough depth to support that goal.

   Once students have had some practice with the ReQuest strategy, they will be able to use it while reading independently. Therefore, if either of the books you select is too long for students to read in class, you may choose to assign portions of the book for homework, using stopping points (see Step 2) to guide the assignments.

2. ***Thoroughly preview the nonfiction text and determine stopping points.*** Students will read this text at the same pace. Determine several places in each chapter at which you'll have students stop reading and *ask you* questions. Choose stopping points in the book at which students are likely to ask *How? Why?* or *What is?* questions about the text, photos, or illustrations.

3. ***Describe or remind students of the purpose of the ReQuest strategy.*** Explain that they will improve their understanding of the book by thinking of questions as they read.

4. ***Introduce the nonfiction text and describe its purpose.*** Before reading *Children of the Wild West*, Davin calls attention to the fact that its primary purpose is to explore the photographs of children taken during the mid to late 1800s as families moved westward across the United States.

5. ***Read aloud to the first stopping point in the text. Then ask students to think of questions that will help them understand what you have read.*** Encourage students to "think like a teacher" and ask you the kinds of questions a teacher might ask. Then answer your students' questions, referring to the text, using prior knowledge, or encouraging discussion among your students in order to do so. In answering students' questions or guiding them toward answers, you are modeling the critical-thinking skills all readers must use as they read.

   During this initial questioning period, Davin's students ask him mostly literal questions about *Children of the Wild West*, such as *What town did they leave from in Missouri? Why hadn't they seen a photograph before? How many children were in the wagon train?* and *Did everybody have kids?*

6. ***Model questions that require more critical thinking, and then ask students to think of these types of questions.*** Davin asks his students: *Why do you think a photographer would want to go west on a wagon train? Why were sentries posted around the camp each evening? Why did the families moving west call themselves emigrants?* Answering these questions requires reasoning, as well as navigating the text to search for answers.

Taking their cue from Davin, his students begin to ask questions that make them think more deeply about the text: *How did a whole family manage to live in the wagon? What did the pioneer boys and girls think about meeting Native Americans for the first time?*

7. **Ask students to read on their own to the next stopping point, and then elicit more questions as well as predictions.** In the nonfiction text, students may find the content hard to predict; however, students may be able to predict what sorts of questions could be answered in the next section. An awareness of the structure of the text is useful in focusing readers' attention and establishing a purpose for further reading.

8. **Continue this process throughout the remainder of the book.** Assign reading for homework if necessary (students can write down their questions at home and bring them to class). To help his students become comfortable with the ReQuest process, Davin varies the reading experience: He reads aloud one chapter and then has students read the next chapter independently.

9. **When the students have completed the nonfiction text, introduce the fiction text.** Predetermine stopping points, as with the nonfiction text. You may use chapter endings as natural stopping points; however, consider stopping after passages students are likely to find challenging, at moments when a character encounters a dilemma or must make an important decision, or after any passage or incident you feel deserves some reflection.

10. **During the question-and-answer periods, encourage students to formulate questions that connect the fiction book with what they learned from the nonfiction book.** For instance, Davin's students ask questions about the differences in the lives of the main character in their fiction text, Teresa Angelino Viscardi, and the children they read about in *Children of the Wild West*. Davin is able to model searching in the nonfiction text for answers to questions about the fiction text.

11. **Evaluate.** After using the ReQuest strategy with both twin books, students should be able to differentiate between the types of questions discussed above; formulate two or three types of questions independently; and answer two or three types of questions by navigating the texts and synthesizing information from both texts.

   To assess their learning, ask students to each create for homework a list of at least five questions about their reading. Only one question may be a literal question. The remaining questions must require inferential thinking, personal reflection, and/or the synthesis of the two texts. Provide examples if necessary.

   Collect and review the students' questions and create a new assignment page that includes at least one question from each student's assignment. This time, ask students to choose three questions to *answer,* only one of which may be a literal question.

Strategy Spotlight: ReQUEST

The Twin Books:

FICTION

West to a Land of Plenty: The Diary of Teresa Angelino Viscardi
by Jim Murphy
(Scholastic, 1998)
(From the Dear America series)

In 1883, Teresa Angelino Viscardi begins both her diary and the long train ride with her family to the unsettled Idaho Territory. Unhappy with her whole family, including her snoopy little sister, she writes about their struggles during the dangerous trip west.

NONFICTION

Children of the Wild West
by Russell Freedman
(Clarion Books, 1983)

This haunting collection of photographs documents the lives of children traveling west with their parents in the early 1800s. Along with the well-written narrative, the photographs help us see into the lives of the children. Readers find out where they lived, what they ate, where they went to school, and how they got along with Native Americans, as well as answers to other questions.

■ Classroom Context

Expanding his fourth graders' critical-thinking skills is a major priority for Davin. As he develops his units of study, he makes a point of planning lessons that call upon students to practice those essential skills.

For social studies, Davin's class studies the westward expansion. Close to the end of the unit he reserves time for students to learn more about the lives of pioneers who traveled west, by looking at the lives of pioneer children. He has found that when his students compare their own lives with those of children from other times, they are highly

motivated and retain more of what they've learned from the entire unit. For this lesson he chooses twin books and the ReQuest strategy to explore the topic.

■ Why These Twin Books?

Davin's students enjoy all the books in the Dear America series, which includes *West to a Land of Plenty*, because they tell the story (in diary form) of children's lives from various periods in history. He often shares the books as Read Alouds, but many students choose to read them during SSR time or as take-home books. In fact, some students now keep their own diaries as a result of reading books from this series.

Children of the Wild West is a natural nonfiction companion book because it describes and has photos of actual westward travelers. The photos keep students grounded in the reality that children just like themselves were among the pioneers; it also provides opportunities to find answers to the questions the fiction text generates.

■ How the Strategy Activity Fits In

Davin wants his students to become critical thinkers and skilled readers as they learn about the westward expansion, so he encourages them to formulate questions about all the material they read in the unit. Prior to their experiences with the twin books, Davin's students read about the westward expansion in their social studies textbooks. He asks them to make notes and record questions about what they read. As a follow-up, he asks groups of three students to discuss the chapter and ask questions of one another about their reading.

Davin asks each small group, *How do you think children were affected by the movement westward?* Because the question focuses on thinking critically about the textbook information, it serves as a model for the type of questions he wants his students to ask one another when they begin using the ReQuest strategy to read the twin books.

■ **Success Story**

The ReQuest procedure and twin-book approach enhance each other in Davin's unit. Beginning with the nonfiction text builds background knowledge about the lives of pioneer children and allows Davin's students to generate a range of questions about what they read. Approaching *West to a Land of Plenty* with a well-established questioning "habit" enriches the students' reading experience and their ability to learn from the book and makes for a seamless integration of information from separate sources.

As the unit concludes, Davin gives his students a variety of opportunities to demonstrate what they've learned. The art projects they produce, which incorporate central concepts, vocabulary, and events studied in the unit, become an excellent source of assessment data for Davin.

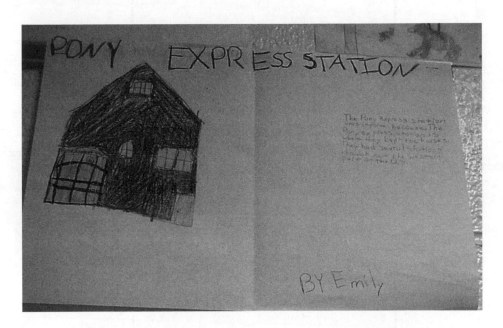

Emily's caption: *The Pony Express station was important because the . . . station is where they kept the horses. They had several stations throughout the western part of the U.S.*

Name _____   Date _____

Fiction Text _____

Nonfiction Text _____

K-W-L Chart

Topic: _____

What I **K**now	What I **W**ant to Know	What I **L**earned

Literature Circle Discussion Skills

Book Title: _____ Date: _____

Pages/Chapters Assigned: _____ Book's Reading Level: _____

Group members	On task	Takes part in discussion	Listens when others speak	Read assignment	Specific job

Overall comments about group:

1 = outstanding

2 = good

3 = needs improvement

CHAPTER 4

Twin-Book Strategies to Enhance Writing

Students who experience the integration of writing and reading are likely to learn more content, to understand it better, and to remember it longer.

—Vacca & Vacca, *Content Area Reading* (1999)

Reading and writing go hand in hand. Your students become better writers by writing extensively, just as they become better readers by reading extensively. The five strategies included in this chapter focus on helping students become better writers through completing different types of writing-response activities. The twin books provide a clear focus on topics that might otherwise be daunting to write about. The fiction engages students by tying content to the students' own lives, and the nonfiction provides reinforcement and answers questions. This solid base encourages students to write—and write with substance.

These strategies also reinforce word recognition and build comprehension as students use the words and ideas they've read about in their writing. The support you offer—through modeling good writing and offering students opportunities to share and get feedback on their writing—helps them become more effective writers.

As you introduce the activities in this section, remind students that even the most talented musicians and athletes must spend many hours practicing and training to reach a high level of expertise. Good readers and writers have to spend lots of time reading and writing. Students can relate to this concept!

VENN DIAGRAM
Comparing and Contrasting to Generate Ideas

OBJECTIVE

First, to deepen students' understanding of a topic or theme by having them compare and contrast selected elements of twin books; second, to use a prewriting organizer to generate thoughtful responses to both texts

HOW IT WORKS

A classic graphic organizer familiar to many teachers, the Venn diagram, constructed of overlapping circles, is used to compare and contrast two or more concepts. Each circle represents one of the concepts. The features that describe one concept exclusively are listed in the nonoverlapping part of that circle; those that describe more than one concept are listed in the area where those circles overlap.

Venn diagrams are excellent companions to a twin-book study because they provide a format for comparing and contrasting any shared element in the twin books: character, setting, structure, voice, author's purpose, and so on. This process supports students' understanding, and the finished diagrams provide a focus and structure for students' writing about the twin books.

WHEN TO USE VENN DIAGRAMS

■ After Reading

Students create diagrams after reading the twin books. The diagrams become the basis for a writing assignment.

PUTTING THE STRATEGY INTO ACTION

The classroom example in this section is from a unit on school integration taught by Edward Zayne. His third-grade students read Amazing Grace *(fiction) and* The Story of Ruby Bridges *(nonfiction); they then use Venn diagrams to compare and contrast the main characters of these books with each other, and later with themselves. (For more on Zayne's unit, see page 70.)*

1. ***Select the twin books.*** Begin by deciding which theme(s) or concept(s) related to the unit you would like students to understand, then choose a set of books that will help illuminate that theme or concept. Zayne wanted to emphasize that children who integrated schools faced tremendous hostility and responded with pride, self-respect, and strength of character. To focus closely on the nature of strength of character, he chose a pair of books with main characters who—although they are not contemporaries, and go to school in different circumstances—share those essential personality traits.

Because it's important that students have both texts fresh in their minds for the Venn diagram strategy, it's a good idea to choose short books that can be read in one or two sittings. Both of Zayne's choices are picture books he can read aloud in a single session.

2. *Read the first text aloud to students or have students read it independently.* Zayne begins with *Amazing Grace,* his fiction book.

3. *Focus students' attention on the concept or theme you want them to explore.* Because Zayne wants his students to think carefully about each book's central character, he starts with a brainstorming session focusing on the character of Grace. He asks students to list Grace's characteristics, feelings, and physical attributes, and he lists these ideas on the board.

4. *Read aloud the second twin book or ask students to read it independently, and hold a similar follow-up discussion.* After reading aloud *The Story of Ruby Bridges,* Zayne asks his students to brainstorm a list of Ruby's characteristics, feelings, and physical attributes and records them as well.

5. *Draw a model diagram on the board for students to copy, labeling the circles to indicate what is being compared or contrasted.* Explain to students what they will be comparing or contrasting and how the Venn diagram works. Zayne labels one circle "Grace" and the other "Ruby."

6. *Compare and contrast the sets of information.* Help students use the Venn diagram to sort the information on the board. In Zayne's class, students go through the lists of characteristics, feelings, and physical attributes, placing commonalities in the area where Grace's and Ruby's circles overlap and differences in the areas where they don't. Zayne completes the class diagram on the board as students complete their own (see photo on the next page).

7. *Use the diagram as a writing prompt.* Ask students to flesh out the ideas in each section of the diagram into paragraphs or essays. They should use examples from the texts to support the descriptive words or phrases from the diagram. Zayne chooses to give his third graders a clear structure for their writing: They will first describe similarities between the two characters, using words from the overlapping sections, and then their differences, using words from the nonoverlapping section.

8. *Evaluate. As you examine students' writing, evaluate their work using questions such as these:*
   Is the written response focused on the theme or concept being explored?
   Has the writer incorporated all the information from the diagram, and with accuracy?
   Does the writer use examples from the text to support the words, phrases, and ideas taken from the diagram?

You may ask students to extend the concept beyond the original diagram by adding a new dimension to the compare/contrast exercise. Zayne's students expanded upon their original writing assignment by adding a third circle to their diagram to represent themselves, so they could compare and contrast their own personal characteristics and circumstances with Grace's and Ruby's. They followed up by adding the new information to the paragraphs they'd already written.

TEACHING TIP
ADDING COMPLEXITY
It is possible to construct Venn diagrams with more than two circles. Consider challenging upper-grade students by drawing several smaller, intersecting circles to compare and contrast more sets of information. Adding circles allows more-experienced students to think divergently.

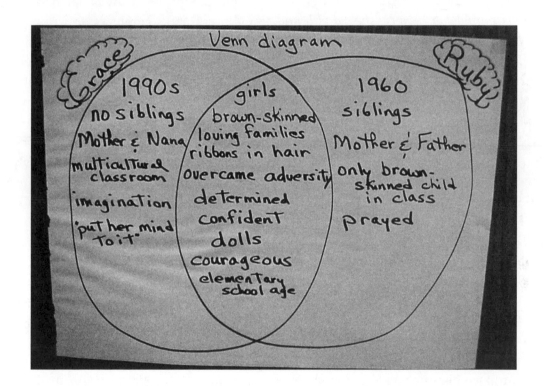

Strategy Spotlight: **VENN DIAGRAM**

The Twin Books:

FICTION

Amazing Grace
by Mary Hoffman
(Scholastic, 1991)

Nana reminds Grace that she can be anything she wants to be. Grace loves to imagine she's someone else. Sometimes she's Joan of Arc, Anansi the Spider, Helen of Troy, Hiawatha, or Mowgli. But most of all she wants to be Peter Pan in the school play. Her friends try to discourage her because she's a girl, and she's black. Nana, however, keeps encouraging Grace not to give up, and she realizes her dream.

NONFICTION

The Story of Ruby Bridges
by Robert Coles
(Scholastic, 1995)

It takes a lot of courage, but 6-year-old Ruby Bridges does it. She is the first black child to attend an all-white elementary school in New Orleans. This is the touching story of the brave little girl who made national headlines in 1960.

■ Classroom Context

There are no children of color in the small, rural school district where Zayne teaches. Zayne makes it a priority to introduce his students to the world outside their own community and often does so through literature. Also impacting his approach to reading and writing are the goals of a districtwide grant to improve writing skills and the statewide test to assess them.

■ Why These Twin Books?

The children respond to the exceptional illustrations in both short picture books; the main characters' expressions are so subtly portrayed that they give students additional insight into Grace's and Ruby's feelings and experiences. Zayne also finds that his students do better with their writing about twin books when he reads books aloud and encourages lots of class discussion. He frequently begins his lessons by asking his students how they are like the children they read about and how they are different. After reading both books, they apply this familiar process to Grace and Ruby. The children always have many comments and questions that provide them with lots of writing material.

■ How the Strategy Activity Fits In

To prepare for the newly adopted state assessment and his district's emphasis on writing, Zayne plans many varied prewriting activities throughout the year. The Venn-diagram exercise is one of these. Zayne has found that the use of graphic organizers improves the quality of his students' writing, and he has introduced several of them to his class, including K-W-L and webbing (see pages 44–48 and 84–89). Zayne believes that once they've organized information on a graphic organizer, students can more easily put that information into structured paragraphs.

During the integration study, Zayne also uses a Venn diagram to teach students about the history of school integration in the United States. He draws the two overlapping circles, labeling one 2005 and the other 1960. Using a Venn diagram to organize two new sets of information and then as a writing prompt reinforces students' understanding of how to compare and contrast as a basis for structured writing.

■ Success Story

After examining his students' writing, Zayne feels confident that his students have gained an understanding of the struggles of black children attending public schools in the South during the 1960s. By comparing Ruby and Grace and then reflecting on their own lives, they have learned that most children have more similarities than differences. They also have learned a powerful tool for organizing information before they write.

DIALOG JOURNAL
A Written Conversation That Digs Deeply Into Texts

OBJECTIVE

First, to provide a forum in which students can respond to literature and in so doing expand and deepen their thinking; second, to provide practice in reading and responding to another person's writing through authentic communication

HOW IT WORKS

There are two types of dialog journals: student-teacher journals and buddy journals. In student-teacher journals, students react to what they've read in a series of entries and submit their dialog journals to you. You respond in writing to their ideas and in the process help them understand how to write meaningfully and appropriately in response to what they've read. Student-teacher journals can serve as a stepping stone to buddy journals, which require more student independence.

In buddy journals, students communicate with one another, reading and responding to a classmates' writing. You monitor the buddy journals, coaching students to help them stay focused and providing mini-lessons or writing prompts as necessary.

WHEN TO USE THE DIALOG JOURNAL

■ **During Reading**

Encourage students to listen or read thoughtfully so that they'll know what they want to communicate in their responses. If you want students to respond to a particular issue or question as they write, you may ask them to read with that purpose in mind.

■ **After Reading**

Discuss the entire selection and ask students to write responses in their journals.

PUTTING THE STRATEGY INTO ACTION

The examples that follow are taken from Lynn Buttram's fourth-grade unit on ancient Egypt. Buttram has selected the twin books Mummy *and* How Would You Survive as an Ancient Egyptian? *to support her students' understanding of life in ancient Egypt. (For more on Buttram's unit, see page 75.)*

1. **Select the twin books.** Choose a fiction book to read aloud and a nonfiction book at students' reading level for them to read independently. Buttram decides to read *Mummy* to her students and provides multiple copies of *How Would You Survive as an Ancient Egyptian?* for them to use as a reference as they write their responses.

2. *Choose the type of journal you will use.* If students are new to journaling and don't have much experience with responding directly to one another in class discussions, begin with student-teacher journals. If, on the other hand, your students have written in response to reading before *and* are adept at listening and responding to one another verbally, you may choose to use buddy journals instead (skip to Step 8).

3. *Make journals with students or supply notebooks for this purpose.* The journal itself may be anything from a professionally bound book to a spiral notebook to copy paper stapled together with construction paper covers. Buttram has her students make their own journals out of colored file folders and lined paper. They cut off the tab on their folder, trim it to better fit the paper, and decorate it for the ancient Egypt theme.

4. *If students are new to writing in response to literature, give them some practice.* Model for students how to respond in writing to a selection read aloud. In addition, to encourage thoughtful writing, plan to discuss what you've read aloud with your class before asking students to write their responses, at least during the first several writing sessions.

   Buttram begins to read *Mummies.* To help students get started with their writing, she asks questions about their thoughts and ideas on what she's read so far. For example, she asks: *What do you think about Emlyn wanting to be a thief? What was the scheme the kids discussed? What do you think about how Emlyn is going to disguise the mummy?* Afterward, she records on chart paper a four- or five-sentence response and has students do the same. She invites students to share their entries and respond to one another's ideas, which builds excitement for writing and helps generate ideas.

5. *Introduce and distribute the nonfiction book to students and explain how they can use it as a reference as they write.* Give students an opportunity to investigate the contents of the book and locate information using the index. Buttram models how to use

TEACHING TIP
E-MAIL JOURNALS
In many classrooms, e-mail journals now replace handwritten ones. Students enjoy using technology because it is challenging, interesting, and different from traditional paper-and-pencil classroom activities. Be sure to exercise all necessary precautions before using this or any other Internet-based student assignment.

TEACHING TIP
PAIRING JOURNAL BUDDIES
Buddies are either selected by students with your approval or assigned. Rotate buddy pairs after about two weeks. This will keep the conversation going and give students a chance to write to everyone in the class. Buttram allows students to choose their own buddy for a couple of rotations because she knows students are more likely to "talk" to someone they already know well.

How Would You Survive as an Ancient Egyptian? to investigate answers to some questions students have raised about *Mummy*. For example, in *Mummy*, two of the main characters hear a rattle inside the mummy. Buttram's students want to find out if that is possible, so they search the nonfiction book and find that bodies were embalmed and wrapped in strips of linen to preserve them. Students conclude that there is nothing living that could be making noise inside a real mummy.

6. ***Begin the written dialogue and establish a schedule for turning in journals.*** Explain to students that you will begin reading their entries and responding to them in writing; Buttram calls it a "conversation in writing" about ancient Egypt. She asks students to write once a week because it takes several days for her to respond to everyone. Students choose which day they want to turn the journal in. She reads it, writes a response, and returns it within two days.

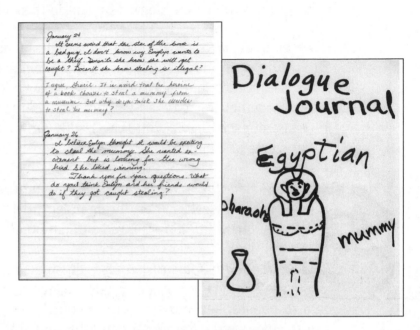

7. ***Support students' writing with your responses.*** Write your comments at the end of the student's response so that the journal is continuous. Focus on developing students' ideas, as well as supporting their written expression. Instead of correcting spelling and grammar, make a point in your response of correctly spelling words students have missed. That way you can make the student feel successful for using the word while demonstrating the correct spelling.

In her responses, Buttram asks questions to help students think critically. For example, Gracie writes: *It seems weird that the star of the book is a bad guy. I don't know why Emlyn wants to be a thief. Doesn't she know she will get caught?* Buttram responds: *I agree, Gracie. It is weird that the heroine of a book chooses to steal a mummy from a museum. But why do you think she decides to steal the mummy?*

In addition, Buttram encourages students to keep stretching themselves by using more-complicated sentence structures and more-sophisticated vocabulary. Every week she chooses one or two of her students' well-constructed sentences to share with the class (she keeps the examples anonymous).

8. ***Prepare students for buddy journals.*** Students can now use their journaling skills with one another. Buttram reminds her students that what they've been doing with her is carrying on a conversation with written, rather than spoken, language.

Ask students to look at their journals and make observations about the types of responses you have written. They may observe, for instance, that you have asked a question for clarification, offered a different perspective, or referred them to the nonfiction text for further research. List these types of responses on a piece of chart paper and keep it posted in the room. When students are ready to respond to one another, encourage them to use the posted list to help them respond appropriately.

As a warm-up to buddy journals, read a selection from the fiction text to your students. Then offer them a written response you've prepared on chart paper or a transparency and ask them to compose a response. Guide them, in particular, to find opportunities to use the nonfiction text in their response.

9. *Have buddies write in their journals.* Buttram asks students to create new journals for writing with buddies. Because buddies change frequently, and each buddy pair starts with a new journal, Buttram uses three sheets of copy paper folded in half and stapled together to create a 5½- by 8-inch journal. Students write their thoughts in the journal and exchange it with their buddy for a response. Each new entry begins where the previous one ended.

10. *Keep the journaling ongoing and easy to manage.* Have students write in the journal once or twice a week, either during independent work time or at home, making sure to allow enough time for you and student buddies to respond.

11. *Review the buddy journals.* After each student has written two entries and two responses and before buddies rotate, collect the journals and review them. Write your own responses, becoming part of the buddy rotation to push students' thinking further and to evaluate their work. When Buttram reads and writes responses in the journals, she is able to evaluate her students' writing growth and plan any needed mini-lessons, such as how to make text-to-self connections, how to ask a writer helpful questions, how to give constructive feedback, and so on.

12. *Discuss the journals with the class.* Listening to selections from classmates' journals gives students even more material to write about in their own. Buttram chooses Fridays for discussions. Keeping the writers' names anonymous, she begins the discussion with some comments students have made in their journals. Since students enjoy listening to one another's ideas about the book, the discussion is lively.

13. *Evaluate.* When you review students' buddy journals, look for these characteristics:

   • Written responses should demonstrate students' understanding of and ability to synthesize information from both texts.

   • Students should respond to the text in a variety of ways, incorporating several response styles you have modeled for the class.

   • Responses should include specific comments or questions that keep the written conversation going.

Strategy Spotlight: **DIALOG JOURNALS**

The Twin Books:

FICTION

Mummy
by Caroline B. Cooney
(Scholastic, 2000)

Emlyn daydreams about being the perfect thief. She doesn't want to harm anyone or use a gun or knife; she just wants to commit the perfect crime. Her friends give her the chance when they decide to steal an Egyptian mummy from a museum.

NONFICTION

How Would You Survive as an Ancient Egyptian?
by Jacqueline Morley
(Scholastic, 2001)

Do you ever wonder how pharaohs spent their days? why Egyptian women shaved one eyebrow? how you'd survive in ancient Egypt? This book has the answers.

■ Classroom Context

Because writing improves students' understanding of any topic, it takes many forms in Buttram's fourth-grade classroom: fictional stories, purposeful letter writing, and reports, to name a few. After attending a presentation about how to integrate journaling into several content areas, Buttram decides to use dialog journaling techniques to support her students' learning about ancient Egypt.

Buttram begins the ancient Egypt unit by engaging her students with educational computer games on that theme. The games generate both excitement and curiosity about ancient Egypt, and Buttram takes advantage of this energy to introduce *Mummy* and begin student-teacher journals.

■ Why These Twin Books?

Buttram chose *Mummy* because facts about ancient Egypt are incorporated into the story: Students learn and remember information easily because it is presented in such an engaging format. The nonfiction book *How Would You Survive as an Ancient Egyptian?* is accessible enough for her students to read independently and includes illustrations that support their comprehension. This book includes a table of contents and index, as well as a short quiz and a useful glossary.

■ How the Strategy Activity Fits In

After playing the educational computer games, listening to *Mummy,* engaging in dialog journaling with the teacher and one another, and using the nonfiction text for further research, Buttram's students are ready to demonstrate their learning in a culminating project. Working with the art teacher, and drawing from all they've learned, Buttram's students create Egyptian-themed artwork they are proud to display in the hall.

■ Success Story

The combination of dialog journaling and twin books supports students' writing and communication skills while they learn about the topic of ancient Egypt. Buttram finds that using the nonfiction book to back up the fiction book helps students sustain high-interest "conversations" in buddy journals. In fact, Buttram has noticed that as her fourth graders gain experience with writing down their thoughts and responding to their classmates' ideas, they begin to use more-complex sentence structures and more-varied vocabulary words than in earlier writing.

Another benefit Buttram has discovered is that spelling improves when she consistently uses journals as part of her students' literacy program. During the course of the written conversation, certain words are used over and over. As a result, her students learn to spell them correctly. In addition, because students are aware that they are writing *to* a reader, they tend to take additional care and present their best work.

DOUBLE-ENTRY JOURNAL
Writing That Invests Students in Their Reading

OBJECTIVE

To encourage students to interact with the texts they read by having them record personal reactions to passages that have special meaning to them

HOW IT WORKS

As students make their way through a text, they keep track of passages that they find interesting or noteworthy. They use a simple graphic organizer to record and briefly respond to these passages. When used in conjunction with twin books, students' responses may include observations about how the two books are related or questions about one book that may be answered by reading the other.

Double-entry journals encourage students to be active readers who can think critically and relate the material they read to their own lives.

WHEN TO USE THE DOUBLE-ENTRY JOURNAL

■ **During Reading**

As students read, they use sticky-notes to mark passages they want to respond to afterward (this allows for uninterrupted reading).

■ **After Reading**

Students go back through the portion of the text they have just read and recopy passages they find meaningful onto the graphic organizer; then they complete the personal response section.

PUTTING THE STRATEGY INTO ACTION

The examples in this section are drawn from a Hiroshima/cultural awareness unit taught by Jared Alexander. His fifth-grade students are learning about the bombing of Hiroshima by reading the twin books Sadako and the Thousand Paper Cranes *and* Hiroshima: A Novella. *(For more on Alexander's unit, see page 79.)*

1. *Select the twin books.* Make sure both books are focused on a key topic you're studying. Try to find a fiction book with a central character with whom your students can identify. Plan to read one of the books aloud, and obtain multiple copies of the other book so that your students can read it independently.

2. *Read the first book aloud to your students over the course of one or more sessions and solicit their responses.* At the end of each Read Aloud session, ask students for their questions and reactions to the book. Offer your own as well, making sure to model several types of responses: those that connect the book to your personal experience (text-to-self); those that connect the text to something else you've read as a class (text-to-text); and those that connect the text to the larger world (text-to-world). Alexander reads aloud to his students *Hiroshima: A Novella.* He encourages them to express their emotional reactions to the text and to ask questions to try to understand the historical context.

3. *Introduce students to the other twin book and give them their copies.* Allow for a very brief discussion of the title, author, and cover illustration. Then give each student a copy of the book and one or two small sticky-notes. Explain to students that as you read the opening of the book, they should follow along in their own books and mark with a sticky-note any passage that inspires them to make a connection.

4. *Read the beginning of the second twin book aloud.* Read the first chapter or enough of the text to help students become invested in the story. Alexander reads the prologue of *Sadako and the Thousand Paper Cranes.*

5. *Introduce the double-entry format.* Close the book (have students do the same) and draw a T-chart on the board to model writing a journal entry. Explain to students that they will use this double-entry journal format to keep track of their thoughts, questions, and reactions to this book.

   Ask a volunteer to share a passage he or she marked with a sticky-note and to explain why he or she did so. Write this passage (or a portion of the passage if it's long) and its page number on the left side of the vertical line on the class chart. On the right, summarize the student's reaction to the passage. Repeat this process once or twice, until you feel your students understand how to use the format.

6. *Have students prepare a sheet of paper to use as a journal page.* Have them divide their paper in half by drawing a line from top to bottom or folding it lengthwise. Keep additional pieces of paper and staplers available so that students can add pages as needed.

7. *Assign students a section of the text to read independently, beginning at the place where you left off in the Read Aloud.* Distribute additional sticky-notes and ask students to put their journals aside as they read; they will write an entry at the end of the session. Alexander asks his students to read independently chapters 1 through 3 and to mark with sticky-notes passages that interest them.

8. *At the end of the session, ask students to respond to two or three of the passages they've marked.* Alexander reminds students that they will recopy the passage (or part

of it) and jot down the page number for reference on the left side of the paper and write their responses on the right.

Alexander instructs his students to avoid simply restating or summarizing the passage. To help students focus on their personal or emotional reactions to the text, he models another sample response to a portion of the prologue:

| p. 7 | **This story is based on the life of a little girl who lived in Japan from 1943 to 1955.** | **My sister was also born in 1943. That would have made Sadako and Paula, my sister, the same age, except Sadako died at age 9.** |

9. *Have students share their journals.* Sharing their journals shows students how personal reading is and deepens their understanding of the subject (see photo below). Alexander gives students many opportunities to share their double-entry journals in small groups and as a class. He continues to encourage different types of responses (see Step 2).

10. *Once students are engaged in the second twin book, encourage them to make connections between this one and the one you read aloud.* Are there questions raised in the first book that are answered by the second one? Does one book provide some context or perspective for the other? Are there inconsistencies between the two books that need explaining? Remind students to include text-to-text connections between the twin books in their journals.

11. **Evaluate.** Collect the journals regularly and read them. Coach students individually by writing suggestions on sticky-notes and attaching them to their journals. As students read the final chapter of the fiction book, prepare a special double-entry journal assignment. Ask them to include three different types of responses (text-to-self; text-to-text, and text-to-world) in their double entry journals for this chapter. Examine their writing to be sure that they understand and use each type of response, and have responded to your coaching.

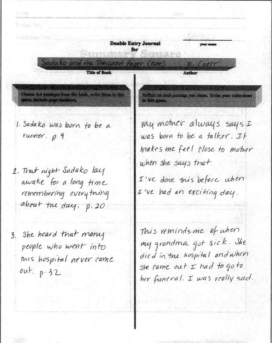

Strategy Spotlight: **DOUBLE-ENTRY JOURNAL**

The Twin Books:

FICTION

Hiroshima: A Novella
by Laurence Yep
(Scholastic, 1995)

This simple narrative lets the reader into the lives of 12-year-old Sachi and her classmates as they witness the impact of the explosion of the atomic bomb on Hiroshima.

NONFICTION

Sadako and the Thousand Paper Cranes
by Eleanor Coerr
(G. P. Putnam, 1977)

Sadako survived the bombing of Hiroshima. However, ten years later leukemia ravaged her body. A Japanese folktale has it that if a sick person folds a thousand paper cranes, that person becomes well. Sadako was able to fold 644. Japanese children still celebrate her bravery.

■ Classroom Context

Alexander, a teacher at a small, suburban school, provides varied opportunities for his students to become aware of other cultures and communities. Studying World War II is part of a larger unit on cultural awareness and understanding. Alexander plans celebrations in honor of special days from several cultures. One such day is Japanese Peace Day, August 6, the day the United States dropped the atomic bomb on Hiroshima in 1945. Alexander uses twin books with double-entry journals to help students understand cultural differences and to teach them to read, think, and write critically.

■ Why These Twin Books?

Alexander wants to provide twin books about World War II that are historically accurate, written at the

reading level of most of his fifth-grade students, and compelling enough to keep their attention. *Hiroshima* is short—a novella of 52 pages—but Yep's descriptions are striking and provoke many questions from students. *Sadako and the Thousand Paper Cranes* shows another side of Japanese culture during and after World War II.

■ How the Strategy Activity Fits In

The state reading assessment Alexander's students must take requires them to read a selection, think critically about a topic, and finally write in a reflective manner about it. During the cultural awareness unit, Alexander uses several sets of twin books along with the double-entry journal strategy to help students practice thinking critically and responding thoughtfully to what they read. In doing so, he is able to focus on the standards while stressing the importance of cultural understanding.

Other twin-book sets Alexander uses in his cultural awareness unit include these:

FICTION: ***Do You Know Me?*** by Nancy Farmer (Scholastic, 1993)

NONFICTION: ***Rehema's Journey: A Visit in Tanzania*** by Barbara Margolies (Scholastic, 1990)

•

FICTION: ***Calling the Doves*** (*El canto de las palomas*) by Juan Felipe (Children's Book Press, 2000)

NONFICTION: ***Mexico and Central America: A Fiesta of Cultures, Crafts, and Activities*** by Mory C. Turck (Chicago Review Press, 2004)

■ Success Story

Alexander has seen that using the double-entry journal with twin books helps his students develop a deep understanding of the topics they study. In addition, through the process of reading and responding to twin books, his students develop the reading comprehension, critical-thinking, and writing skills they need to be successful on the state assessment instrument.

GROUP SUMMARIZING
Focused Writing to Learn Content Information

OBJECTIVE

To improve students' listening and reading comprehension skills and to teach them to summarize information in an accurate, organized way

HOW IT WORKS

Researchers link students' comprehension and retention of information with their ability to accurately summarize it (Olson & Gee, 1991). To orchestrate a group summary, a teacher reads aloud to students or assigns reading on a specific topic. The teacher then helps students sort and categorize the information contained in the selection, identifying the main ideas, salient concepts, and most important facts (and distinguishing these from supporting details). As a class, students compose a summary of what they've read. This process supports students' understanding of the topic. In addition, since this is a group activity, it reinforces social skills such as listening to others, speaking in turn, and respecting others' opinions.

WHEN TO USE GROUP SUMMARIZING

■ After Reading

Group summarizing is an effective after-reading writing activity. As students articulate and revise their individual summaries with peer support, they reinforce what they've learned from their reading and practice writing their ideas clearly and concisely. They can easily translate summary sentences into topic sentences for report writing.

PUTTING THE STRATEGY INTO ACTION

The following examples are taken from a fourth-grade Antarctica unit taught by Alex Deraj. Deraj teaches his students to summarize information, using the twin books Polar Wildlife *and* Playing With Penguins and Other Adventures in Antarctica. *(For more on Deraj's unit, see page 83.)*

1. *Select the twin books.* The twin books you choose for group summarizing should be short, high-interest selections on the same topic. Make sure to narrow the scope of the topic so students can focus on summarizing skills as they learn. For instance, Deraj's students study polar wildlife as part of their Antarctica unit, but the twin-book activity focuses on penguins exclusively.

    Look for twin books with clear, information-rich writing. You may consider using picture books or books that feature prominent illustrations, so that students can practice summarizing skills by writing captions for the pictures. Have enough twin books available so that each pair of students has access to a set of twin books.

2. **Model summarizing skills.** Read aloud a paragraph from the nonfiction book. Guide students in identifying the important facts in the paragraph and stating them in sentence form. Explain what *summarizing* means: Deraj asks his students to imagine how they would tell a friend quickly about a whole movie without repeating all the dialogue, line for line. Students practice summarizing several paragraphs from the book as single sentences. Deraj records these sentences on the board and points out all the details the students have (correctly) left out.

3. **Choose four categories for students to research as they read.** To give students a purpose and focus for reading, identify four kinds of information for them to search for. Create a simple graphic organizer to keep the categories separate. Deraj chooses Description, Food, Home, and Interesting Facts. He divides a piece of chart paper into four sections and labels them with these headings.

4. **Return to the section you and your students have read (from Step 2) and ask students in which category the information belongs.** Deraj's students decide that since the information they found is about the polar environment, they should put it under the heading Home.

5. **Pair up students and give each pair a set of twin books and each student a copy of the Summary Square reproducible (page 90).** Deraj asks each pair to begin by reading a short selection about Antarctica from their social studies textbook. After they finish, he gives the students the option of reading on their own or in pairs and allows them to decide which twin book to read first.

6. **Give students time to read and summarize information, then sort it into the categories on the graphic organizer.** As Deraj's students work, some of them write phrases; others write complete sentences. This research part of the lesson lasts about 25 to 30 minutes. Members of some pairs trade books with each other or read one book, then the other, together.

7. **For each of the four categories, ask for a volunteer to write a summary statement.** Create a large four-column chart on the board. As they listen, to their classmate's responses, volunteers rephrase and write summary statements in sentence form on the class chart.

Group summarizing—class chart			
Description	**Food**	**Home**	**Interesting Facts**
Penguins are birds, but they can't fly. Penguins are good divers and swimmers.	Penguins eat fish, squid, and krill.	Penguins spend lots of time swimming. Many penguins don't build nests.	Penguins use the same rookery every year. Penguins don't all look the same. They lose their feathers every year and grow new ones.

8. ***Encourage discussion.*** Ask students where individual pieces of information came from, and draw their attention to information that was garnered by synthesizing the content of *both* twin books. Typical comments from some of Deraj's students are "I didn't know there were so many different kinds of penguins. The twin books showed lots of different ones" and "Penguins walk funny, but the books said they were good swimmers." Students will use the summaries for writing in the next step.

9. ***Ask students to write about what they learned about the topic, with the summary statements on the class chart as a guide.*** Depending on your students' experience with writing, you may decide to ask them to write a simple paragraph or a three-paragraph essay incorporating what they have learned. Have students focus their paragraphs on one of the categories from the chart and link the summary statements in the column together in an organized and logical way. More-sophisticated writers may use the summary statements in a column as topic sentences for the paragraphs of their essays and then add supporting details they've read and recorded.

10. ***Evaluate.*** To assess your students' ability to summarize, synthesize, and explain in writing their understanding of what they've read, give them a two-part homework assignment to complete individually. On the first night, assign two brief readings on the same topic. Ask students to read the texts and use a summary sheet to sort what they've learned into the categories you've given them. In school the next day, take a few minutes to answer questions raised by the reading; also solicit a few sample summary statements from students. Let students add missing information—with a colored pencil, so you will recognize these additional notes as you review the assignment—to their graphic organizers if they wish. Then send them home with the graphic organizers, asking them to incorporate their learning into a paragraph or an essay, as appropriate.

As you review the completed assignments, take note of how much information students were able to summarize and sort on their own, and what they added with the help of the class. Then examine their writing to see whether students have created summaries that use original, full sentences; are logically organized; and remain focused on the main points of the text they have read. Use the information you learn from reviewing the assignments to inform your teaching in the next group summarizing lesson.

Strategy Spotlight: **GROUP SUMMARIZING**

The Twin Books:

FICTION

Playing With Penguins and Other Adventures in Antarctica
by Ann McGovern
(Scholastic, 1994)

This informative book about penguins and other Antarctic animals is written in diary format from the point of view of one man's journey to the cold, frozen land.

NONFICTION

Polar Wildlife
by Kamini Khanduri
(Scholastic, 1992)

From the popular Usborne series, this book contains fascinating facts and illustrations about many species of wildlife in the polar lands.

■ Classroom Context

Deraj loves to teach about Antarctica. He visited the icy continent on one of his trips to Australia and since that time has been gathering books, videos, and other information to enhance the unit. His students are fascinated with his stories and artifacts from Antarctica. He successfully links the study to several district and state standards and engages his students in an intriguing study of the strange, distant land.

■ Why These Twin Books?

Deraj's social studies textbook contains some material about Antarctica, and he has chosen to use twin books to expand upon that information and enrich the study. His students enjoy the photographs in *Playing With Penguins* as well as the diary format of the text, which is written in short, yet complete sentences. In *Polar Wildlife* short, fact-based paragraphs are set close to companion illustrations, providing

manageable sections for students to summarize in a sentence or two.

■ How the Strategy Activity Fits In

Before beginning the Antarctica unit, Deraj displays posters, copies of the twin books, and other related books all over the room, generating excitement among his students. After writing paragraphs on several subtopics regarding penguins, they go on to write reports that synthesize all the penguin categories they've researched.

As the unit continues, Deraj's students begin to see how the details of a narrower topic (penguins) fit into a larger topic (polar wildlife), and how that in turn fits into a broader topic (Antarctica). Students work in small groups to study other wildlife of Antarctica and draw comparisons between animals native to that continent. Students ask many questions about how polar animals survive in zoos in the United States. Out of that discussion comes the idea to write to a zookeeper for answers. Deraj presents a mini-lesson on letter writing that emphasizes the importance of revising to make sense of confusing ideas and writing respectfully to a professional audience. Students use their summary statements to make sure their letters are accurate, share some of what they know, and pose questions about what they want to know. Deraj's students are surprised and delighted when the class receives answers to their questions from several zoos.

■ Success Story

Both the group summarizing activity and the correspondence with people from zoos around the country are authentic writing activities. In composing purposeful writing, Deraj's students successfully read for information, synthesize information from various sources, and restate ideas in an organized, thorough way. Deraj believes his students retain a great deal more from the unit than they would without the summarizing and writing activities.

WEBBING
Organizing Information for Report Writing

OBJECTIVE

First, to help students identify the main topic and then subtopics in texts they read; second, to teach students how to use a web organizer to plan and write a report.

HOW IT WORKS

The teacher reads aloud a set of twin books, both focused on the same topic. He or she then helps students decide on the main topic of both texts and sort the supporting information into subtopic categories. The main topic and subtopics are graphically represented as a web, with the main topic at the center and the subtopics radiating out from the center. Each subtopic can be graphically connected to smaller subtopics.

WHEN TO USE WEBBING

■ Before Reading

While webbing is primarily used during and after reading, it is possible to use webbing to help students *predict* what will be included in a text. This is useful if you wish to direct students' attention to how a nonfiction book is organized or to encourage students to ask questions before they read.

■ During Reading

While they read, students can create a web, putting the central topic or theme in a middle circle and filling in the radiating circles with subtopics or key ideas.

■ After Reading

Students may complete a web after they read as a prewriting activity to reinforce learning and support reading comprehension.

PUTTING THE STRATEGY INTO ACTION

The following examples are drawn from a unit focused on heroes and heroines in American history taught by Ellie Bartlett. She begins her unit with George Washington, choosing the twin books George Washington's Breakfast *(fiction) and A Picture Book of George Washington *(nonfiction), both of which she will read aloud to her class. (For more on Bartlett's unit, see page 88–89.)*

1. ***Select the twin books.*** Biographies are great nonfiction choices for this strategy; select a companion fiction book that provides more information about the historical period or setting portrayed in the biography, or even one that uses a historical figure as a

character. Be sure that both books contain accurate information and are relatively short, high-interest selections you can read aloud in one or two sessions. If you are working with more mature readers, you may choose a fiction selection that takes longer to read as long as it engages your students and they retain a lot of the story. If you choose to do this, read the fiction selection first.

2. **Read the books aloud to your class, one at a time.** Over the course of several days, Bartlett reads aloud both texts.

3. **Begin the webbing activity.** Ask students to name the central topic the books share. Write the central topic in the center of a piece of chart paper. Circle it and add radiating lines for supporting ideas or subtopics. At the end of each line, write the name of a subtopic and circle it.

   In Bartlett's lesson, the topic is George Washington. She writes the topic in the center of the web and has students brainstorm categories of information they've learned about Washington's life from their reading. Bartlett suggests that they organize the information chronologically, based on stages or eras in Washington's life. With that prompt, Bartlett's students suggest naming the supporting categories Birth, Youth, Adulthood, and Death. She adds one word to the end of each line on the web organizer and circles it (see photo below).

4. **Ask students to volunteer information to fill in the web.** Fill in details by adding more radiating lines from the subtopic circles, writing the information volunteered by students at the ends of the lines, and circling them. To generate details, Bartlett asks her students, *What are the basic facts of Washington's birth and death? What are the important things to know about his youth? What were the major events of George Washington's adulthood?*

5. **Use the information in the web to write a report as a class.** Ask students to begin at the center of the web and make broad statements about the topic. Her students volunteer: *George Washington was a famous man, We know a lot about George Washington, I would like to be like George Washington,* and *George Washington was a hero.* Bartlett thinks aloud, synthesizing these four statements. She begins the report this way: *George Washington was a famous man, and we know a lot about him. Many people want to be like him because he was a hero.* She records this statement on chart paper for the class and has them copy the model as she writes it. (They will refer to this example when they write their own reports later in the unit.)

6. **Break down the process, paragraph by paragraph.** Show students how to use the subtopics from the second-tier circles to form individual paragraphs and the specific information included in the third-tier (outer) circles to add detail sentences. As Bartlett continues using the model as an aid for the focused writing, she tells students that each circle connected to the central topic is material for a separate paragraph about a period in the life of George Washington. As they write together, she refers to the twin books to check and clarify the information they used for the web.

7. **Have students summarize the topic to create a conclusion.** Bartlett explains that the purpose of a conclusion is to wrap things up for the reader and that some conclusions include a final, summarizing thought that echoes the opening paragraph. Then she guides her students in creating a conclusion for their class essay.

8. **Ask students to pair up and select a new twin-book set and then repeat the webbing process with new categories.** Have a variety of short twin books available for this purpose. Pair students up and allow each set of partners to choose which twin-book set they'd like to read. Ask students to be creative in the way they organize the information from the twin books. Circulate as students work, observing the ways in which each pair of readers is structuring their web. Stop the class occasionally to share these alternative structures, encouraging students to experiment and be flexible.

> ## George Washington
>
> George Washington was a famous man, and we know a lot about him because he was a hero.
> Washington was born in Virginia on February 22, 1732. His family lived on a farm.
> When he wa a boy, he liked to go fishing and boating in a river close to his home. He also really liked to ride horses.
> He married Martha Curtis who had 2 children and lots of money.
>
> After they married, they moved to Mt. Vernon.
> Washington was asked to be the leader of the Continental Army. While he was in the Army, he became a hero to everyone. We know him best as our 1st President.
> George Washington died in 1799. He is still a hero.

9. *Ask students to use their webs to write a report.* Bartlett tells her students to include information from both texts in their reports and to stretch phrases or brief notes on the web into full sentences by adding details from the outermost circles of the web. Finally, she reminds them that as they write they can refer to the class web and report. Because students write the reports individually, Bartlett makes copies of webs made in partnerships as needed.

10. *Evaluate.* Examine students' reports, looking for several features:

- The report should contain information learned from both twin books, and the information contained in the report should reflect an understanding of both texts.

- The report should be organized coherently, and subtopics should be explained with supporting details from the web.

- Thoughts in the report should be stated in complete sentences with appropriately complex sentence structure.

Strategy Spotlight: **WEBBING**

The Twin Books:

FICTION

George Washington's Breakfast
by Jean Fritz
(Scholastic, 1969)

George Washington Allen is proud of his name and wants to know all about his namesake. He wants to know what George Washington wore, what he ate, where he lived—absolutely everything about the first president.

NONFICTION

A Picture Book of George Washington
by David A. Adler
(Holiday House, 1989)

This biography picture book about George Washington spans his life from childhood to his death in 1799.

■ Classroom Context

For the past 24 years, Bartlett has ended the school year with a study of heroes and heroines in American history. The unit has become part of her school's history.

Bartlett loves sharing children's literature with students and uses twin books for most of the heroes and heroines study—students make a strong connection with their heroes through the fiction books and are able to absorb a lot of information from the nonfiction books. She also finds that the webbing strategy supports students' understanding of the lives of heroes they study and provides a helpful organizer for report writing.

■ Why These Twin Books?

Bartlett uses the fiction book to awaken and retain students' interest in the first president. Students are surprised by how much they learn about George

Washington as the main character of *George Washington's Breakfast*, George Washington Allen, tries to discover what Washington ate for breakfast. Bartlett chooses *A Picture Book of George Washington* as its companion book because it provides a basic, factual schema of his life. She often uses picture books as the nonfiction selections so that her students can read them quickly and independently.

■ How the Strategy Activity Fits In

At the beginning of Bartlett's monthlong focus on heroes and heroines in American history, she demonstrates the webbing strategy with the twin books about George Washington. She talks briefly about other famous people, mentioning other twin books, including the following:

FICTION: *Abraham Lincoln's Hat* by Martha Brenner (Random House, 1994)

NONFICTION: *A Picture Book of Abraham Lincoln* by David A. Adler (Holiday House, 1990)

•

FICTION: *Mr. Revere and I* by Robert Lawson (Little, Brown & Co., 1998)

NONFICTION: *Paul Revere's Ride* by Shana Corey (Random House, 2004)

•

FICTION: *Ben and Me* by Robert Lawson (Little Brown & Co., 1988)

NONFICTION: *Ben Franklin of Old Philadelphia* by Margaret Cousins (Random House, 2004)

•

FICTION: *My Dream of Martin Luther King* by Faith Ringgold (Dragonfly Books, 1998)

NONFICTION: *Martin's Big Words! The Life of Dr. Martin Luther King, Jr.* by Doreen Rappaport (Hyperion, 2001)

Bartlett tells students that they'll write reports on one individual. She asks them to each keep a list of famous Americans they might like to write about at the end of the unit. After they've finished their study, each student decides on one individual from his or her list to study in depth. Then Bartlett provides twin books and other chapter books for students to read in order to gain more information.

As part of the unit, Bartlett's students also create cardboard puppets of their historical figures and write biographical summaries to go with them (see photo below). These are posted around the room. With parents' help and contributions, Bartlett offers period costume pieces to match the heroes they've studied. Students put the pieces together to create period costumes to wear for a special event: a Hero and Heroine Party where students present their hero and biography. The twin books are also on display during the party for parents to look at while they enjoy simple snacks.

■ **Success Story**

During the course of the unit, Bartlett's students demonstrate through their webs, research reports, artwork, and class discussions that they have learned a great deal about heroes and heroines in American history. They also show through their writing that they can read, comprehend, and organize information in a new way with a web and then synthesize it into a well-written, factual report.

Name _____   Date _____

Fiction Text _____

Nonfiction Text _____

Summary Square

Topic: _____

In the boxes below, summarize the information you learned.

Twin Books Recommended in the Classroom Examples

FICTION	NONFICTION
Postcards from Pluto: A Tour of the Solar System by Loreen Leedy	*Do Stars Have Points?* by Melvin and Gilda Berger
Survival! Fire by K. Duey and K.A. Bale	*The Great Fire* by Jim Murphy
A picture of Freedom: The Diary of Clotee, a Slave Girl by Patricia McKissack	*Rosa Parks: My Story* by Rosa Parks with Jim Haskins
Thunder on the Tennessee by G. Clifton Wisler	*A Nation Torn: The Story of How the Civil War Began* by Delia Ray
Woodrow, the White House Mouse by Peter W. Barnes & Cheryl Shaw Barnes	*The Race for President* by Leigh Hope Wood
Harriet and the Promised Land by Jacob Lawrence	*Wanted Dead or Alive: The True Story of Harriet Tubman* by Ann McGovern
Stellaluna by Janell Cannon	*Bats* by Celia Bland
Anna Is Still Here by Ida Vos	*A Place to Hide: True Stories of Holocaust Rescues* by Jayne Pettit
The Long Way to a New Land by Joan Sandis	*Coming to America: The Story of Immigration* by Betsy Maestro
West to a Land of Plenty: The Diary of Teresa Angelino Viscardi by Jim Murphy	*Children of the Wild West* by Russell Freedman
Amazing Grace by Mary Hoffman	*The Story of Ruby Bridges* by Robert Coles
Mummy by Caroline B. Conney	*How Would You Survive as an Ancient Egyptian?* by Jacqueline Morley
Hiroshima: A Novella by Laurence Yep	*Sadako and the Thousand Paper Cranes* by Eleanor Coerr
Playing With Penguins and Other Adventures in Antarctica by A. McGovern	*Polar Wildlife* by Kamini Khanduri
George Washington's Breakfast by Jean Fritz	*A Picture Book of George Washington* by David A. Adler

Please contact Deanne Camp at DeanneCamp@missouristate.edu for a list of additional twin-book recommendations.

Professional Sources Cited

Blachowicz, C. (1986). Making connections: Alternatives to the vocabulary notebook. *Journal of Reading, 29,* 643–649.

Camp, D. (2000). It takes two: Teaching with twin texts of fact and fiction. *The Reading Teacher, 53,* 400–408.

Camp, D. (2001). READ: A comprehension strategy using children's literature. *The Missouri Reader, 26*(1), 3–15.

Carr, E., & Ogle, D. (1987). KWL plus: A strategy for comprehension and summarization. *Journal of Reading, 30,* 626–631.

Gillet, J., & Kita, M. J. (1979). Words, kids and categories. *The Reading Teacher, 32,* 538–542.

Harris, T. L., & Hodges, R. E. (Eds.). (1995). *The literacy dictionary: The vocabulary of reading and writing.* Newark, DE: International Reading Association.

Hurst, B., Wilson, C., Camp, D., & Cramer, G. (2002). *Creating independent readers: Developing word recognition skills in K–12 classrooms.* Scottsdale, AZ: Holcomb Hathway.

International Reading Association & National Council of Teachers of English (1996). *Standards for the English language arts.* Newark, DE: IRA; Urbana, IL: NCTE.

Klemp, R. M. (1994). Word storm: Connecting vocabulary to the student's database. *The Reading Teacher, 48,* 282.

Manzo, A. V. (1969). The ReQuest procedure. *Journal of Reading, 13,* 123–126, 163.

Muhall, M. (1992). Kinderjournals. *The Reading Teacher, 45,* 738–739.

National Reading Panel. (2000). *Report of the National Reading Panel: Teaching children to read. Report of the subgroups.* Washington, DC: U.S. Department of Health and Human Services, National Institutes of Health. Retrieved May 2006 from http://www.nichd.nih.gov/publications/nrp/findings.htm

National Research Council. (1996). *National science education standards.* Washington, D.C.: National Academy Press.

Norton, D. (1992). Modeling inferencing of characterization. *The Reading Teacher, 46,* 64–67.

Ogle, D. M. (1986). K-W-L: A teaching model that develops active reading of expository text. *The Reading Teacher, 39,* 564–570.

Olson, M. W,. & Gee, T. C. (1991). Content reading instruction in the primary grades: Perceptions and strategies. *The Reading Teacher, 45,* 298–307.

School reform: Getting it right. (1994). *American Educator, 18*(3), 12–13.

Schwartz, R. M., & Raphael, T. E. (1985). Concept of definition: A key to improving students' vocabulary. *The Reading Teacher, 39*, 198–205.

Stauffer, R. G. (1969). *Directing reading maturity as a cognitive process*. New York: Harper & Row.

Vacca, R. T., & Vacca, J. L. (1999). *Content area reading: Literacy and learning across the curriculum* (6th ed.). New York: Longman.

Wood, K. D., & Robinson, N. (1983). Vocabulary, language, and prediction: A pre-reading strategy. *The Reading Teacher, 36*, 392–395.

Children's Books Cited

Adler, D. (1989). *A picture book of George Washington*. New York: Holiday House.

Adler, D. (1990). *A picture book of Abraham Lincoln*. New York: Holiday House.

Barnes, P. W., & Barnes, C. S. (1998). *Woodrow, the White House mouse*. New York: Scholastic.

Berger, M., & Berger, G. (1998). *Do stars have points?* New York: Scholastic.

Bland, C. (1996). *Bats*. New York: Scholastic.

Brenner, M. (1994). *Abraham Lincoln's hat*. New York: Random House.

Cannon, J. (1993). *Stellaluna*. San Diego: Harcourt Brace.

Coerr, E. (1977). *Sadako and the thousand paper cranes*. New York: G. P. Putnam.

Coles, R. (1995). *The story of Ruby Bridges*. New York: Scholastic.

Cooney, C. B. (2000). *Mummy*. New York: Scholastic.

Corey, S. (2004). *Paul Revere's ride*. New York: Random House.

Cousins, M. (2004). *Ben Franklin of Old Philadelphia*. New York: Random House.

Duey, K., & Bale, K. A. (1988). *Survival! Fire*. New York: Aladdin Paperbacks.

Farmer, N. (1993). *Do you know me?* New York: Scholastic.

Felipe, J. F. (2000). *Calling the doves (El canto de las palomas)*. San Francisco: Children's Book Press.

Freedman, R. (1983). *Children of the Wild West*. New York: Clarion Books.

Fritz, J. (1969). *George Washington's breakfast*. New York: Scholastic.

Fritz, J. (1994). *Around the world in a hundred years*. New York: Penguin Putnam.

Hoffman, M. (1991). *Amazing Grace*. New York: Scholastic.

Khanduri, K. (1992). *Polar wildlife*. New York: Scholastic.

Lawrence, J. (1997). *Harriet and the promised land*. New York: Aladdin.

Lawson, R. (1988). *Ben and me*. New York: Little, Brown & Co. (Original work published 1939)

Lawson, R. (1998). *Mr. Revere and I*. New York: Little, Brown & Co. (Original work published 1953)

Leedy, L. (1993). *Postcards From Pluto: A tour of the solar system*. New York: Scholastic.

Levine, E. (1993). *If you traveled on the underground railroad*. New York: Scholastic.

MacDonald, F. (1988). *Magellan: A voyage around the world*. Danbury, CT: Franklin Watts.

Maestro, B. (1996). *Coming to America: The story of immigration*. New York: Scholastic.

Maestro, B. and Maestro, G. (1992). *The discovery of the Americas*. New York: Harper Trophy.

Margolies, B. (1990). *Rehema's journey: A visit in Tanzania*. New York: Scholastic.

McGovern, A. (1965). *Wanted dead or alive: The true story of Harriet Tubman*. New York: Scholastic.

McGovern, A. (1994). *Playing with penguins and other adventures in Antartica*. New York: Scholastic.

McKissack, P. (1997). *A picture of freedom: The diary of Clotee, a slave girl*. New York: Scholastic.

Morley, J. (2001). *How would you survive as an ancient Egyptian?* New York: Scholastic.

Murphy, J. (1998). *West to a land of plenty: The diary of Teresa Angelino Viscardi*. New York: Scholastic.

Parks, R. (with Haskins, J.) (1992). *Rosa Parks: My story*. New York: Scholastic.

Pettit, J. (1993). *A place to hide: True stories of Holocaust rescues*. New York: Scholastic.

Polacco, P. (1994). *Pink and Say*. New York: Philomel Books.

Rappaport, D. (2001). *Martin's big words! The life of Dr. Martin Luther King.* New York: Hyperion.

Ray, D. (1990). *A nation torn: The story of how the Civil War began.* New York: Scholastic.

Ringgold, F. (1998). *My dream of Martin Luther King.* New York: Dragonfly Books.

Sandis, J. (1986). *The long way to a new land.* Minneapolis, MN: Sagebrush Educational Resources.

Sansevere-Dreher, D. (1992). *Explorers who got lost.* New York: Tor Books.

Turck, M. C. (2004). *Mexico and Central America: A fiesta of cultures, crafts, and activities.* Chicago: Chicago Review Press.

Vos, I. (1986). *Anna is still here.* New York: Scholastic.

Wisler, G. C. (1983). *Thunder on the Tennessee.* New York: Scholastic.

Wood, L. H. (2000). *The race for president.* Chicago: KidBooks.

Yep, L. (1995). *Hiroshima: A novella.* New York: Scholastic.

Index